NOTABLE CHILDREN'S films and videos, filmstrips, and recordings, 1973–1986

prepared by

Notable Films, Filmstrips, and Recordings, 1973–1986 Retrospective Task Force
Association for Library Service to Children
American Library Association

American Library Association
Chicago and London 1987

Cover designed by Bernie Kagel

Text designed by Marcia Lange

Printed on 50-pound Glatfelter, a pH neutral stock, and bound in 10-point Carolina cover stock by Thomson-Shore
♾

Library of Congress Cataloging-in-Publication Data

Notable children's films and videos, filmstrips, and recordings, 1973-1986.

Includes indexes.
1. Moving-pictures for children--Catalogs. 2. Filmstrips in education--Catalogs. 3. Sound recordings in education--Catalogs. I. Association for Library Service to Children. Notable Films, Filmstrips, and Recordings, 1973-1986 Retrospective Task Force.
PN1998.N76 1987 011'.37 87-14395
ISBN 0-8389-3342-4

Contents

Preface

PURPOSE

The Association for Library Service to Children, a division of the American Library Association, established a Film Evaluation Committee in 1973, a Recording Evaluation Committee in 1975, and a Filmstrip Evaluation Committee in 1976. The purpose of these committees, consisting of ALSC members, is to identify high quality, noteworthy films, filmstrips, and recordings for children and to recognize their excellence by designating them "notable."

The three committees operate in a similar manner. Individual committee members preview films, filmstrips, and recordings prior to meeting as a group. When the committees meet as a whole, the members view the materials again, deciding which should be designated "notable." The criteria for selection are listed below.

Each year new lists of notable materials are released. The lists have been published in Top of the News, Booklist, and School Library Journal. The current lists are published together in a brochure by School Library Journal.

However, there has never been a compilation of all past lists. Such a compilation, containing a complete listing of notable films, filmstrips, and recordings, along with current prices and formats, may serve as a useful tool in collection building and as a historical record of these exemplary materials.

A committee of three persons (Teresa Poston Heyser, Norman, Oklahoma; Lynne R. Pickens, Atlanta, Georgia; and Hilda Weeks Parfrey, Madison, Wisconsin) was appointed to create this annotated master list of all notable materials.

CRITERIA

Each ALSC committee which evaluates films, filmstrips, or recordings uses the following criteria. The materials selected as "notable" are of especially commendable quality. They reflect respect for the child's intelligence and imagination, exhibit venturesome creativity, and, in exemplary ways, reflect and encourage children's interests. Aesthetic and technical aspects are considered as are the effective use of voices, music, language, sound effects, and in the case of films and filmstrips, visuals, which, taken together, create a unified whole. If the materials are adaptations, they remain true to, expand, or complement the original work while meeting the general criteria for excellence. Materials which are appropriate for children from preschool through age 14 are considered.

AVAILABILITY

To determine availability of these materials, the committee members contacted the producers and/or distributors for each item. When the committee members received no reply from the producer or distributor, the item was labeled "Availability unknown." Some items are no longer in stock; these were labeled "No longer available." Libraries are encouraged to use interlibrary loan to obtain items unavailable for purchase. Of the 159 films, 80 filmstrips, and 180 recordings designated as "notable," over 90 percent are still available for purchase. Thus, libraries and schools which wish to develop collections of "notables" should find most items available.

ARRANGEMENT

The films, filmstrips, and recordings are listed alphabetically by title in separate lists. Brief annotations and buying information have been supplied. The information is the most recent obtainable at the time of complilation. Following the master lists are a directory of distributors and indexes of subjects, authors, illustrators, and performers.

ENTRY

The entry consists of the title, the producer (when known), the author or performer, the distributor, the copyright or release date (when known), the format (e.g., phonodisc, cassette, filmstrip, videocassette), the product number (when available), the purchase price, the rental price (where applicable), the length in minutes (when available), and the grade levels for which the material is suitable. All items are in color unless otherwise noted. Materials are generally available for preview, usually to qualified buyers. The distributor should be contacted to obtain an item for preview. The entry is followed by a brief annotation.

INDEXES

Indexes to subjects, authors, performers, and illustrators are provided. The films, filmstrips, and recordings are listed together under the appropriate subject. Individual performers on recordings may be accessed through the Index to Performers. The Index to Authors provides access to authors of the books on which the films, filmstrips, and recordings are based. A brief Index to Illustrators lists the names of illustrators of books which have been made into films or filmstrips when the illustrator is not the same as the author.

ACKNOWLEDGMENTS

The editor gratefully acknowledges the assistance from many people in the preparation of this publication. The cooperation from the distributors of the films, filmstrips, and recordings is appreciated. Lynne R. Pickens and Teresa Poston Heyser were conscientious and highly valued committee members. Gail Sage, past president of the Association for Library Service to Children, Jane Botham, current president of the association, Ann Carlson Weeks, former Executive Director of ALSC, and Susan Roman, present Executive Director of ALSC, all lent enthusiastic support to the project. Ron Goral, librarian of the Instructional Materials Selection Center, Madison Metropolitan School District, Wisconsin, provided invaluable assistance to the editor, as did Joanne Lenburg, Educational Reference Librarian, Madison Metropolitan School District. Eliza Dresang, Manager of Media Services, Madison Metropolitan School District, was a constant source of support. Lastly, the editor wishes to thank her husband, Rick Parfrey, for his interest in the project as well as his good will, advice, and assistance throughout.

Hilda Weeks Parfrey

Key to Abbreviations

av.	average
ea.	each
F	film
fr.	frames
FS	filmstrip
fs	filmstrips
I	intermediate level; for children in grades 4-6
J	junior level; for children in grades 6-up
min.	minutes
mm	millimeters
P	primary level; for children in grades K-3
pb.	paperback
Pr	preschool level; for children in grades K-3
R	recording
video	videocassette

Sample Entries

FILM AND VIDEO

Title — Producer — Date — Running time

3 Angel and Big Joe. Bert Salzman. 1975. 27 min.

Format — Sale price — Format — Sale price — Rental price

16mm: $500 (EW451). Video: $350 (EW451). Rental: $50.

Producer's serial number

Learning Corporation of America. (I-J).

Distributor — Grade level

FILMSTRIP

3 Ben's Trumpet. Random House. 1980. (#394-66059-5).

1 fs, 110 fr. with cassette. 11:08 min. $27.50.

Random House. (P-I-J).

RECORDING

Title — Performer

2 ALBERTA SINGS. Performed by Suni Paz and friends.

Producer — Date — Phonodisc or cassette — Sale price — Running time

Folkways. 1980. Phonodisc (FC7830) $9.98. 47 min.

Producer's serial number

Folkways. (P-I-J).

Distributor — Grade level

Notable Films and Videos

1 ALL AT SEA. Hugh Stewart and Kenneth Fairbarn. 1974. 60 min. Sterling Educational Films. (I-J). No longer available.

A group of English children on a school cruise becomes involved in the theft of a valuable museum painting in this live-action film filled with wild chases, hair-raising escapes, and slapstick humor.

2 THE AMAZING COSMIC AWARENESS OF DUFFY MOON. Daniel Wilson. 1976. 32 min. 16mm: $500 (F2070). Video: $200 (V1796). Rental: $50. Time-Life Video. (I-J).

Pint-sized Duffy develops self-confidence through a mail-order course in "cosmic awareness." This entertaining film successfully blends humor, suspense, and a realization that there's nothing wrong with being different. The film is based on Jean Robinson's The Strange but Wonderful Cosmic Awareness of Duffy Moon (Seabury, 1974).

3 ANGEL AND BIG JOE. Bert Salzman. 1975. 27 min. 16mm: $500 (EW451). Video: $350 (EW451). Rental: $50. Learning Corporation of America. (I-J).

The friendship between Big Joe, the telephone lineman, and Angel, a young Chicano migrant worker, reaches a turning point when Angel must decide between his family and Big Joe.

4 ANIMATION PIE. Robert Bloomberg. 1974. 27 min. Film Wright. (I-J). Availability unknown.

A fresh and lively film on animation uses the work of children from the Mt. Diablo School District Film Workshop to illustrate such techniques as drawing on film, pixilation, clay animation, use of cutouts, and construction of flip books.

5 APPLE DOLLS. Bernard B. Sauerman for Labyrinth Films. 1979. 19 min. 16mm: $350. Video: $175. Rental: $35. Wombat Productions. (I-J).
This introspective film combines the mechanics of the folk craft of carving apple dolls with a philosophical statement about the relationship between the art of handcrafts and the art of living.

6 AQUARIUM. Perspective Films. 1978. 10 min. 16mm: $250 (3859). Video: $175 (3859). Rental: $40. Coronet Film & Video. (P-I-J).
The wonder of unusual sea creatures is captured in exquisite color photography accompanied by a musical score that emphasizes each creature's uniqueness. Identifying information for this non-narrated film is provided by film notes.

7 ARROW TO THE SUN. 1973. 12 min. 16mm: $240 (974-0003). Video: 3/4": $149 (974-6003); 1/2": $99 (974-9003). Rental: $40. Films, Inc. (P-I-J).
The artistic themes of the Acoma Pueblo culture are richly woven in stylized, animated art which portrays a young boy's journey to find his father, the sun. The film is based on Gerald McDermott's Caldecott award-winning book, Arrow to the Sun (Viking, 1974).

8 BALLET ROBOTIQUE. Bob Rogers. 1982. 8 min. 16mm: $225 (1234). Video: $225 (1234). Rental: $60. Pyramid Film & Video. (P-I-J).
Special lighting and multi-screen images expand synchronized robots on an assembly line into a stunning corps de ballet, dancing four movements of "Ballet Robotique" to the accompaniment of the London Royal Philharmonic Orchestra.

9 THE BAMBOO BRUSH. Atlantis Films. 1983. 26 min. 16mm: $575. Video: 3/4": $174; 1/2": $149. Rental: apply. Beacon Films. (I-J).
Benjamin, a Chinese-American teenager, cannot see any reason for studying Chinese until his grandfather shows him a new way of looking at life.

10 BEARSKIN. Tom and Mimi Davenport. 1983. 19:30 min. 16mm: $350. Video (both VHS and Beta): $60. Rental: $35. Davenport Films. (P-I).
The Appalachian Mountain setting contributes to the folk nature of the Grimm Brothers' tale in this live-action adaptation of a story of conflict between good and evil in which a young man is challenged to a surprising test of endurance.

11 THE BEAST OF MONSIEUR RACINE. Weston Woods. 1974. 9 min. 16mm: $215 (MP160). Video (both VHS and Beta): $50 (MPV160). Rental: $20/day. Weston Woods. (P).
Monsieur Racine tames a charming, lumpish animal of unknown origin, eventually taking it to the Academy of Sciences in Paris for identification; a riot ensues, leaving Paris in an uproar. This animated cartoon is adapted from the book by Tomi Ungerer (Farrar, 1971).

12 BOOKER. Avon Kirkland. 1984. 40 min. 16mm: $699. Video: $524. Walt Disney Educational Media. (I-J).
An inspiring dramatization of young Booker T. Washington's determination to learn to read is portrayed in this live-action film.

13 A BOY, A DOG, AND A FROG. John Sturner and Gary Templeton for Evergreen. 1981. 9 min. 16mm: $210 (20172). Video: $145 (20172). Rental: $20. Phoenix Film & Video. (Pr-P-I).
An elusive frog leads a small boy and his dog on a merry chase. This film is a humorous, non-narrated dramatization of the book by Mercer Mayer (Dial, 1967).

14 A BOY AND A BOA. Lora Hays. 1975. 13 min. 16mm: $265 (20150). Video: $175 (20150). Rental: $25. Phoenix Film & Video. (I-J).
Nigel, a young boy's pet boa constrictor, escapes in the local public library, causing great excitement among the stunned patrons.

15 THE BRIDGE OF ADAM RUSH. Daniel Wilson. 1975. 47 min. 16mm: $700 (F1918). Video: $200 (V1517). Rental: $70. Time-Life Video. (I-J).
Twelve-year-old Benjamin moves from colonial Philadelphia to a farm when his widowed mother remarries. Initial resentments between stepfather and stepson disappear as they cooperate to build a much-needed bridge.

16 THE BRONZE ZOO. Sonya Friedman. 1974. 16 min. 16mm: $315 (974-0004). Video: 3/4": $198 (974-6004); 1/2": $142 (974-9004). Rental: $55. Films, Inc. (P-I-J).
The filmmaker follows sculptor Shay Rieger through the creative process as she discusses her work, forms animal figures from plaster, and ultimately has them cast in bronze.

17 BURT DOW, DEEP WATER MAN. Morton Schindel. 1983. 10 min. 16mm: $215 (MP262). Video (both VHS and Beta): $50. Rental: $20/day. Weston Woods. (Pr-P).

Burt Dow, a salty ol' deep water seaman from Maine, puts out to sea in his leaky Tidely-Idley and meets a whale. Based on the book by Robert McCloskey (Viking, 1963), this animated film captures the atmosphere of a New England fishing village.

18 BUTTERFLY. Nico Crama, Holland. 1975. 4 min. 16mm: $125. Video: 3/4": $125; 1/2": $95. Rental: $15/day. Carousel Film & Video. (I-J).

This animated film tells the story of the last butterfly on earth as it fights urbanization and pollution. The powerful ending and effective musical background make this much more than "just another ecology film."

19 THE CAP. Atlantis/National Film Board of Canada. 1984. 25 min. 16mm: $575. Video: 3/4": $174; 1/2": $149. Beacon Films. (I).

The loss of an autographed baseball cap precipitates a conflict between father and son.

20 THE CASE OF THE ELEVATOR DUCK. Learning Corporation of America. 1974. 17 min. 16mm: $350 (EE442). Video: $275 (EE242). Rental: $30. Learning Corporation of America. (P-I).

In this live-action film, Gilbert, an imaginative young detective, tries to find the owner of a duck which is riding the elevator in Gilbert's housing project. The film is based on the book by Polly Berrien Berends (Random House, 1973).

21 CASTLE. Unicorn Productions. 1983. 58 min. (full length). 34 min. (edited version). 16mm: $745 (full length); $480 (edited version). Rental: $100 (full length); $50 (edited version). Lucerne Films. Video: $300 (full length); $200 (edited version). PBS Video. (I-J).

The story of the building of a fictional thirteenth-century Welsh castle is told through a combination of animation, photography of actual castles, drawings from David Macaulay's Caldecott Honor Book (Houghton, 1977), and narration describing castle life.

22 CECILY. Kratky Films, Prague. 1974. 7 min. 16mm: $150. Video: $120. Rental: $25. Learning Corporation of America. (P-I).

This animated film portrays the story of a girl whose long ears enable her to fly away from her cruel grandmother to Africa where she befriends the elephants and forms an elephant orchestra to accompany her vocal solos.

23 CHANGES, CHANGES. Morton Schindel. 1973. 6 min. 16mm: $175 (MP154). Video (both VHS and Beta): $50 (MPV154VC). Rental: $20/day. Weston Woods. (Pr-P).
Two imperturbable wooden dolls move blocks to form a building, a fire engine, a train, etc., in response to fire, flood, and other difficulties in this lively, non-narrated animated film. The film is based on the book by Pat Hutchins (Macmillan, 1971).

24 CHARLIE NEEDS A CLOAK. Morton Schindel. 1977. 8 min. 16mm: $175 (MP167). Video (both VHS and Beta): $50 (MPV167). Rental: $20/day. Weston Woods. (Pr-P).
Charlie, a hard-working shepherd, makes the wool from his sheep into a much-needed red cloak. With the help of an embarrassed freshly shorn sheep and a lilting musical score, this animated film is based on the book by Tomie dePaola (Prentice-Hall, 1973).

25 CHICK CHICK CHICK. Dimension Films. 1975. 12:50 min. 16mm: $240. Video: $170. Rental: $40. Churchill Films. (Pr-P-I-J).
Sequences of a hatching egg punctuate the fast-paced, non-narrated film of chicks and barnyard life. Bluegrass music and natural animal sounds complement the excellent photography.

26 CHILDREN OF THE FIELDS. Bob Young. Guidance Associates. 1973. 20 min. 16mm: $425 (FO4309). Video (both VHS and Beta): $149 (VO4309). Lucerne Films. (I-J).
This documentary reveals the sad and difficult life of ten-year-old Nena Galinda, one of five children in a Chicano migrant family. There is no narration or musical background. The natural sounds of work, play, and conversations communicate the plight of memorable, compelling people.

27 A CHRISTMAS GIFT. Will Vinton. 1980. 8 min. 16mm: $225. Video: $112.50. Rental: $40. Billy Budd Films. (Pr-P-I-J).
A homeless boy shares his meager rations with a solitary old woman to create a warm and memorable Christmas Eve. Superbly detailed clay animation brings life to the ballad "Christmas Dinner."

28 CHRISTMAS LACE. Ko-Zak Productions, Inc. 1978. 27 min. 16mm: $520 (3632). Video: $415 (VC3632). Rental: $52. Encyclopaedia Britannica Educational Corporation. (I-J).
A desperate thief is affected by a young lacemaker's gift in this beautifully photographed Christmas film set in nineteenth-century Quebec.

29 CLAYMATION. Will Vinton. 1978. 18 min. 16mm: $350 (1001). Video: $350 (1001). Rental: $55. Pyramid Film & Video. (I-J).
A behind-the-scenes look at the techniques and procedures of Will Vinton's unusual clay animation. This imaginative production also features clips from some of his well-known films.

30 THE CLOWN OF GOD. Ball and Chain Studios. 1982. 10 min. 16mm: $215 (MP260). Video (both VHS and Beta): $50 (MPV260). Rental: $20/day. Weston Woods. (P-I).
A background of Renaissance music enhances this animated adaptation of Tomie dePaola's book (Harcourt, 1978) which tells the legend of a juggler whose last performance was for the Holy Child on Christmas Eve.

31 THE CONCERT. Mark O'Connor. 1975. 12 min. 16mm: $275 (0750). Video: $275 (9750). Rental: $45. Pyramid Film & Video. (Pr-P-I-J).
In this zany fantasy, the black and white stripes of a London pedestrian crosswalk become the keyboard of a piano for the steps of mime Julian Chagrin.

32 CORDUROY. Joe Mantegna and Gary Templeton for Evergreen/Firehouse Productions in association with Weston Woods. 1984. 16 min. 16mm: $315. Video: $50. Weston Woods. (Pr-P).
This live-action film uses delightfully innovative techniques to bring Don Freeman's popular story (Viking, 1968) of the bear without a button to life.

33 CORNET AT NIGHT. Michael MacMillan, Seaton McLean, and Janice Platt for Atlantis Films. 1984. 25 min. 16mm: $575. Video: 3/4": $174; 1/2": $149. Beacon Films. (I-J).
A cornet player from the city brings a new dimension to the harsh lives of a Midwestern farm family in the 1930s. The film is based on a short story by Sinclair Ross.

34 CRAC. Frederic Back, Societe Radio-Canada. 1981. 15 min. 16mm: $350 (1177). Video: $350 (1177). Rental: $55. Pyramid Film & Video. (P-I-J).

Lyrical French-Canadian folk music complements the crayon-texture animation of this wordless, light-hearted story of a rocking chair and its owners.

35 THE CREATION. Will Vinton. 1981. 9 min. 16mm: $225. Video: $112.50. Rental: $40. Billy Budd Films. (I-J).

Innovative use of clay painting techniques, James Earl Jones's superb narration, and eloquent mood music result in a sensitive, yet powerful interpretation of James Weldon Johnson's classic poem, "The Creation."

36 CURIOUS GEORGE. Churchill Films. 1984. 14 min. 16mm: $320. Video: $225. Rental: $40. Churchill Films. (Pr-P).

The curious little monkey's misadventures are portrayed in this puppet animated film based on H. A. Rey's book (Houghton, 1941).

37 CURIOUS GEORGE GOES TO THE HOSPITAL. Churchill Films. 1983. 15 min. 16mm: $355. Video: $250. Rental: $40. Churchill Films. (Pr-P).

Curious George, the playful monkey, creates havoc in the hospital in this puppet animation of the story in H. A. and Margret Rey (Houghton, 1966).

38 DEAF LIKE ME. Jim Callner. 1981. 23:30 min. 16mm: $495 (A309). Video: $495 (A309). Rental: $49.50. Barr Films. (P-I-J).

The gift of friendship and the treasures of mime bring a special joy to the soundless world of a lonely young girl in this realistic drama.

39 DINOSAUR. Will Vinton/Pyramid Films. 1980. 14 min. 16mm: $325 (1097). Video: $325 (1097). Rental: $55. Pyramid Film & Video. (P-I-J).

Classmates' attention wanes as Philip gives his report on dinosaurs, until the prehistoric animals come to life through claymation in this humorous, engaging, and informative film.

40 DOGS, CATS, AND RABBITS. 1973. 7 min. 16mm: $195 (975-0013). Video: 3/4": $149 (975-6013); 1/2": $99 (975-9013). Rental: $35. Films, Inc. (Pr-P).

Three imaginative and very short films are combined: 41 Barks, "drawn and barked by Eliot Noyes, Jr."; Catsup, Tana Hoban's film of playful kittens; and Rabbits, in which filmmaker Bill Stitt renders rabbits in media ranging from sugar cubes to peanut-butter-and-jelly sandwiches.

41 DRAGON OVER THE HILL. Moreland-Latchford. 1977. 8 min. 16mm: $175 (4027). Video: $99.95 (4027). Rental: $25. AIMS Media. (P-I-J).
Animated metal sculptures portray the story of two blacksmiths and their encounter with a firebreathing dragon.

42 DUDH KOSI: RELENTLESS RIVER OF EVEREST. Guild Sound and Vision. 1982. 27 min. 16mm: $850 (HC1211,16). Video: $230 (HC1211,VS). Rental: $40. Indiana University Audio-Visual Center. (I-J).
The technically superior photography of this documentary captures the drama and suspense as seven courageous adventurers kayak down the treacherous, boulder-filled white waters of the world's steepest river.

43 THE FABLE OF HE AND SHE. Learning Corporation of America. 1974. 11 min. 16mm: $250 (EK441). Video: $175 (EK441). Rental: $25. Learning Corporation of America. (P-I).
Intense color and original use of clay and velvet animation highlight this appealing tale which challenges stereotyped and sexist thinking and celebrates the joys of individual self-expression.

44 FIRE! Film Polski. 1977. 9 min. 16mm: $225 (3562). Video: $225 (VC3562). Rental: $22.50. Encyclopaedia Britannica Educational Corporation. (P-I-J).
This film is an eloquent presentation of life in a forest--at first tranquil, then quickly ravaged by fire, and ultimately promising rebirth. Created by brilliant manipulation of oil paint on glass, the film is enhanced by dramatic music and natural sounds.

45 THE FLASHETTES. Bonnie Friedman and Emily Parker Leon. 1977. 20 min. 16mm: $375. Video: $350. Rental: $45. New Day Films. (I-J).
An upbeat documentary of an inner city girls' track club shows how, through hard work and dedicated coaching, the young women gain pride and self-discipline as well as medals.

46 FLIGHT OF ICARUS. Julien Bryan. 1974. 6 min. ACI Media. (I-J). Availability unknown.
In this animated adaptation of the film Sunflight, the myth of

Daedalus and Icarus is given brief and poetic narration while striking symbolic images convey the drama and essence of the story.

47 FLOATING FREE. Jerry Butts. 1978. 11 min. 16mm: $250 (1022). Video: $250 (1022). Rental: $50. Pyramid Film & Video. (P-I-J).
Exciting action photography of the 1977 World Frisbee Championships provides an enjoyable celebration of the skillful prowess of both humans and canines.

48 FLOWERS IN THE SAND. Christine Cornish and Leon Marr. 1981. 28 min. 16mm: $475 (22153). Video: $275 (22153). Rental: $45. Phoenix Film & Video. (I-J).
The story of a mentally retarded young man who gains the courage to move toward independence through his friendship with a twelve-year-old girl is sensitively depicted in this thought-provoking film.

49 THE FOOLISH FROG. Bill Bernal. 1973. 8 min. 16mm: $195 (MP149). Video (both VHS and Beta): $50 (MP149VC). Rental: $20/day. Weston Woods. (Pr-P-I).
A bouncy musical tall tale, sung by Pete Seeger, tells about the time the whole town, including the cows, chickens, barns, and brook, visited the corner store to celebrate a frog's exploits and drink strawberry soda and eat soda crackers. It is based on the book by Pete and Charles Seeger (Macmillan, 1973) illustrated by Miloslav Jagr.

50 FOOTSTEPS ON THE CEILING. David Gelfand. 1981. 8 min. 16mm: $190 (22152). Video: $125 (22152). Rental: $18. Phoenix Film & Video. (P-I-J).
A young girl's feelings and reactions as she grieves for her dying grandmother are poignantly portrayed in this wordless film.

51 FREE TO BE ... YOU AND ME. Marlo Thomas and Carole Hart for the MS Foundation. 1974. 42 min. 16mm: $695 (620077). Video: $525 (104770). Rental: $75. CRM/McGraw-Hill Films. (P-I-J).
Sexism and sexist attitudes are explored in a series of live-action and animated short stories in this ground-breaking film which features a host of celebrities.

52 THE FUR COAT CLUB. Linda Gottlieb. 1973. 18 min. 16mm: $350 (LEE131). Video: $250 (LEE131). Rental: $35. Learning Corporation of America. (P-I).

In this live-action film, non-narrated and filled with suspense and humor, two girls, who devote their afternoons to stalking people in furs and keeping score of how many they touch, find themselves accidentally locked in a furrier's vault for the night.

53 HANK THE CAVE PEANUT. Yellow Bison Productions. 1974. 15 min. 16mm: $320. Video: 3/4": $174; 1/2": $149. Rental: apply. Beacon Films. (P-I).
An apprentice canoe builder (an animated peanut) must earn his place in the peanut clan by capturing a wild fork in this original non-narrated film.

54 HANNAH AND THE DOG GHOST. Ken Harrison. 1981. 30 min. 16mm: $485 (22179). Video: $280 (22179). Rental: $45. Phoenix Film & Video. (I-J).
A masterful blend of music and photography intensifies this haunting retelling of an Afro-American folktale in which Hannah and her young son encounter the evil fiddleman.

55 HARDWARE WARS. Ernie Fosselius and Michael Wiese. 1978. 13 min. 16mm: $325 (1449). Video: $325 (1449). Rental: $55. Pyramid Film & Video. (I-J).
Princess Ann Droid and Fluke Starbucker take on the giant waffle iron in the sky and battle a toaster in this nuts-and-bolts satire of Star Wars.

56 HAROLD'S FAIRY TALE. Morton Schindel. 1974. 7:45 min. 16mm: $175 (MP158). Rental: $20/day. Weston Woods. (Pr-P).
In this adaptation of Crockett Johnson's picture book (Harper, 1952), Harold's purple crayon creates and transforms his world into an enchanted garden plagued by an invisible giant witch.

57 HE MAKES ME FEEL LIKE DANCIN'. Emile Andolino for Edgar J. Scherick Assoc. 1984. 51 min. 16mm: $850. Video: $250. Rental: $100. Direct Cinema. (I-J).
Jacques D'Amboise of the New York City Ballet introduces school children to the joys of dance in this inspiring and entertaining celebration of talent and determination.

58 THE HIGHWAYMAN. Granada Television of England. 1974. 14 min. Eccentric Circle Cinema Workshop. (P-I-J). Availability unknown.
Sam, with the help of his magic ball, foils the attempts of a dreaded highwayman who tries to hold up a stagecoach in this action-packed British film filled with subtle humor and colorful animation.

59 A HOME RUN FOR LOVE. Martin Tahse. 1979. 47 min. 16mm: $700 (F2160). Video: $200 (V1932). Rental: $70. Time-Life Video. (I-J).
Admiration for Jackie Robinson and passion for the game cement the friendship of fatherless white boy and an older black man during the 1947 baseball season. The film is based on the book by Barbara Cohen, Thank You, Jackie Robinson (Lothrop, 1974).

60 HOUDINI NEVER DIED. Insight Productions. 1979. 28 min. 16mm: $505. Video: $255. Rental: $50.50. Wombat Productions. (I-J).
Magicians old and young continue the spirit and magic of Master Harry Houdini. Original footage of Houdini's daring escapes is included.

61 THE HUNDRED PENNY BOX. Churchill Films. 1979. 16mm: $340. Video: $240. Rental: $40. Churchill Films. (I-J).
This beautifully created film captures the essence of many special moments shared by a young boy and his hundred-year-old aunt as she uses her penny box to tell stories from her life that correspond to the year of the penny. The film is based on the Newbery Honor Book by Sharon Bell Mathis (Viking, 1975).

62 I'LL FIND A WAY. National Film Board of Canada. 1977. 26 min. 16mm: $465. Video: $225. Rental: $45. The Media Guild. (I-J).
Though physically handicapped by spina bifida, nine-year-old Nadia considers herself to be an ordinary child, and her honesty and confidence convince others to see her this way too.

63 I'M A MAMMAL AND SO ARE YOU. National Film Board of Canada. 1980. 4 min. 16mm: $120. Video: $120. Rental: $20. Benchmark Films. (Pr-P-I-J).
Common characteristics of mammals are cleverly presented using verse and catchy hoedown-flavored music synchronized with live-action footage.

64 I'M FEELING ALONE. Churchill Films. 1974. 8 min. 16mm: $170. Video: $120. Rental: $40. Churchill Films. (P).
This live-action film illustrates a variety of situations in which young children can feel sad and lonely.

65 IT MUST BE LOVE 'CAUSE I FEEL SO DUMB. Arthur and Evelyn Barron. 1976. 29 min. 16mm: $500 (EE961). Video: $350 (EE961). Rental: $50. Learning Corporation of America. (I-J).
Thirteen-year-old Eric, a loner, tries to change his personality to impress his first love. When his dog is killed, a girl, who likes him the way he is, provides the compassion he needs.

66 IT'S SO NICE TO HAVE A WOLF AROUND THE HOUSE. Learning Corporation of America. 1979. 12 min. 16mm: $250 (EE192). Video: $175 (EE192). Rental: $25. Learning Corporation of America. (Pr-P-I).
An elderly man and his three very old pets are invigorated when their household is joined by a charmingly efficient wolf with a shady past in this animated adaptation of Harry Allard's picture book (Doubleday, 1977).

67 ITZHAK PERLMAN--IN MY CASE MUSIC. Tony DeNonno. 1982. 10 min. 16mm: $250. Video: $225. Rental: $35. Arthur Mokin Productions, Inc. (I-J).
An intimate portrait of violinist Perlman is presented; he shares the joy of his music, the love of his family, and his concern for the physical and emotional needs of the handicapped.

68 THE JUGGLING MOVIE. Patrick Melly. 1980. 10 min. 16mm: $215. Video: $215. Rental: $25. Little Red Filmhouse. (P-I-J).
Members of the Pickle Family Circus demonstrate juggling to children and showcase their skills in a comedic routine.

69 KATURA AND THE CAT. Lillian Moats and J. P. Somersaulter/Perspective Films. 1982. 11 min. 16mm: $255 (4187). Video: $180 (4187). Rental: $40. Coronet Film & Video. (P-I).
This original fairy tale tells of Katura's encounter on Halloween Eve with the evil forest witch. The distinctive use of animated black-and-white images provides a dramatic background for the touches of color and heightens the eerie atmosphere.

70 KICK ME. Robert Swarthe. 1976. 8 min. 16mm: $190. Video: $190. Rental: $25. Little Red Filmhouse. (P-I-J).
A chase, so heated that the film finally appears to burn, is the subject of this brightly colored and swiftly paced animation drawn on film. A jaunty pair of legs kick at objects in their path until they are in turn pursued by a giant ball, a fish, and a horde of spiders.

71 KUUMBA: SIMON'S NEW SOUND. Nguzo Saba Films. 1978. 8 min. 16mm: $160. Video: 3/4": $174; 1/2": $149. Rental: apply. Beacon Films. (Pr-P-I).
This animated film portrays the story of Simon, who uses his creativity to invent the steel drum at carnival time in Trinidad. Animated by American teenage women, this film is one of a series highlighting the seven African principles of unity.

72 LEGEND OF JOHN HENRY. Pyramid/Bosustow. 1974. 11 min. 16mm: $295 (1752). Video: $295 (1752). Rental: $45. Pyramid Film & Video. (I-J).
John Henry pits his strength against a steam drill to prove that he is truly a steel-driving man in this powerfully animated visual experience accompanied by Roberta Flack's rhythmic blues.

73 LIFE TIMES NINE. Insight Productions. 1973. 15 min. 16mm: $325. Video: 3/4": $195; 1/2": $95. Rental: $45. Pyramid Film & Video. (J).
Nine samples of a "commercial for life," created by students eleven to sixteen years old with the help of professional actors and film crews are presented. Their irreverent approaches to "selling life" utilize a wide variety of film and story techniques.

74 THE LILITH SUMMER. Bernard Wilets. 1984. 28 min. 16mm: $545 (9779). Video: $395 (9779). Rental: $50. AIMS Media. (I-J).
Ellen, 11, and Lilith Adams, 77, are hired to take care of each other one summer; their relationship is portrayed in this sensitive drama about adolescence and aging based on the novel by Hadley Irwin (Feminist Press, 1979).

75 THE LITTLE PRINCE. Will Vinton. 1979. 27 min. 16mm: $550. Video: $275. Rental: $40. Billy Budd Films. (I-J).
Using sophisticated claymation, the integrity and spirit of Saint-Exupery's classic story (Harcourt, 1943) is translated into an exhilarating visual adventure.

76 LITTLE RED RIDING HOOD: A BALINESE-OREGON ADAPTATION. 1980. 17 min. 16mm: $350 (975-0031). Video: 3/4": $198 (975-6031); 1/2": $142 (975-9031). Rental: $55. Films, Inc. (P-I).
The natural beauty of an Oregon forest and the use of Balinese-inspired masks and music highlight this wordless retelling of the classic folktale.

77 LITTLE TIM AND THE BRAVE SEA CAPTAIN. Morton Schindel. 1976. 9 min. 16mm: $215 (MP47). Rental: $20/day. Weston Woods. (Pr-P).

Edward Ardizzone's story (Walck, 1955) of a small boy's adventures as a stowaway and of his heroism in a storm at sea is effectively portrayed in this iconographic work.

78 LUKE WAS THERE. Learning Corporation of America. 1977. 32 min. 16mm: $500 (EW461). Video: $350 (EW461). Rental: $50. Learning Corporation of America. (I-J).

When twelve-year-old Julius must spend some time at a children's shelter, he takes with him his fear and suspicion of adults. This effective and touching dramatization of the book by Eleanor Clymer (Holt, 1973) focuses on the growing relationship between Julius and his counselor, Luke, who helps the boy understand that some adults do care.

79 LULLABY. Csonka Cyorgy/Pannonia Films. 1977. 3:30 min. 16mm: $110 (IFB707). Rental: $7.50. International Film Bureau. (Pr-P).

Toys and other objects from a child's world drift through surrealistic dreamlike scenes illustrating a poem by Atilla Jozsef. This animated film is backed by a soothing lullaby sung in Hungarian.

80 THE MAGIC HAT. Nick DeNoia. 1980. 23 min. 16mm: $365 (620452-9). Video: $260 (107788-Y). Rental: $50. CRM/McGraw-Hill Films. (I).

An upbeat musical, sung and danced by a multi-ethnic cast of youngsters, features a magic hat, a message of self-worth, and a sparkling performance by the young male lead.

81 MAN FROM NOWHERE. Jean Hadlow. 1978. 60 min. 16mm: $745. Rental: $74.50. Lucerne Films. (I-J).

When orphan Alice comes to live with her wealthy great-uncle, the sinister "man from nowhere" appears, warning her to leave Tower House at once.

82 THE MARBLE. Jan Oonk. 1973. 10 min. Pyramid Film & Video. (I-J). No longer available.

This film is an imaginative fantasy in which a boy recovers his magic cat's eye marble from villains, braving a horde of soldiers and artillery to rescue it. Without dialogue, this is a subtle, sophisticated live-action film with an eerie, dreamlike quality.

83 ME AND DAD'S NEW WIFE. Daniel Wilson. 33 min. 16mm: $500 (F2060). Video: $200 (V1788). Rental: $50. Time-Life Video. (I-J).

When Nina, a twelve-year-old whose parents are divorced, discovers her math teacher is her father's new wife, she uses her friends to punish the new wife. The film is based on the book A Smart Kid Like You by Stella Pevsner (Seabury, 1974).

84 ME AND YOU KANGAROO. Learning Corporation of America. 1974. 19 min. 16mm: $350 (EE441). Video: $250 (EE441). Rental: $35. Learning Corporation of America. (P-I).

This live-action film accompanied by aboriginal music presents the story of a young Australian boy's devotion to his pet kangaroo, sensitively portraying the conflicts and emotions that go with responsibility, love, and sacrifice.

85 MEMORIAL DAY. Michael Vlick. 1984. 16mm: $295. Video: $100. Rental: $30. Direct Cinema. (P-I-J).

This film of an actual Memorial Day celebration highlights the people, the parade, and the feelings associated with this small-town tradition.

86 METAMORPHOSIS. 1977. 10 min. 16mm: $210 (975-0034). Rental: $40. Films, Inc. (P-I-J).

In an unusual combination of science and mood photography, a young girl prepares for and scientifically observes the metamorphosis of a caterpillar into a butterfly. A quiet musical background augments this live-action, non-narrated film.

87 MIGHTY MOOSE AND THE QUARTERBACK KID. Harry Bernsen and Alex Karras. 1977. 31 min. 16mm: $500 (F1953). Video: $200 (V1816). Rental: $50. Time-Life Video. (I-J).

Twelve-year-old Benny wants most of all to take pictures, but his football-crazed father insists that Benny become a star quarterback.

88 MIRACLE OF LIFE. Sveriges Television, Sweden. 1983. 57 min. 16mm: $850 (F2610). Video: $250 (V2728). Rental: $85. Time-Life Video. (I-J).

Lennart Nilsson's fibre-optic photography inside the human reproductive system illustrates beautifully the wonder of conception and birth.

89 MR. FROG WENT A-COURTING. National Film Board of Canada. 1973. 5 min. 16mm: $140 (101-0075). Video: 3/4": $95 (101-60075); 1/2": $95 (101-90075). Rental: $35. Films, Inc. (Pr-P).

Elegant animated cutouts illustrate the traditional folk song sung to a lute accompaniment.

90 MISTER GIMME. Learning Corporation of America. 1979. 28 min. 16mm: $500 (EW192). Video: $350 (EW192). Rental: $50. Learning Corporation of America. (I-J).

Tony learns you can't get rich quick in this live-action film set in an Italian-American neighborhood in Brooklyn.

91 THE MOLE AS PAINTER. Kratky Films, Prague. 11 min. 16mm: $235 (20015). Video: $140 (20015). Rental: $16. Phoenix Film & Video. (P).

Animals decorate themselves with painted patterns to frighten off the fox in a tale presented in lively animated images.

92 THE MORNING SPIDER. Mark O'Connor. 1976. 22 min. 16mm: $395 (2065). Video: $395 (2065). Rental: $60. Pyramid Film & Video. (P-I-J).

A zany "bug's-eye" view of insect life, imaginatively costumed and mimed by Julian Chagrin and troupe, is presented in this wordless film.

93 MORRIS'S DISAPPEARING BAG. Morton Schindel. 1982. 6 min. 16mm: $175 (MP230). Video (both VHS and Beta): $50 (MPV230). Rental: $20/day. Weston Woods. (Pr-P).

Morris discovers a magical Christmas gift that enables him to make his brothers and sisters disappear, giving him a chance to enjoy their presents. The film is based on the book by Rosemary Wells (Dial, 1975).

94 MY MOTHER NEVER WAS A KID. Learning Corporation of America. 1980. 30 min. 16mm: $500 (EP081). Video: $350 (EP081). Rental: $50. Learning Corporation of America. (I-J).

Victoria hits her head in a subway and is transported back in time. There she encounters her mother as a teenager and gains a new perspective about her mother. The film is based on the book <u>Hangin' Out with Cici</u> by Francine Pascal (Archway, 1978).

95 MY WORLD ... WATER. Paul Fillinger Films. 1974. 11 min. 16mm: $185. Video: $185. Churchill Films (P).

In a documentary that explores the wonders and uses of water, expressions of concern by children regarding water conservation create an ecological focus.

96 NATURE ADVENTURE. Universal Education. 1975. 14 min. Universal Education. (P-I-J). No longer available.
A lone man in a canoe photographs and records the animals and birds of the wilderness in this live-action film with no narration.

97 NICKY: ONE OF MY BEST FRIENDS. Togg Films. 1976. 15 min. 16mm: $255 (620177). Video: $195 (107630-1). Rental: $25. CRM/McGraw-Hill Films. (I-J).
Blind and partially paralyzed, twelve-year-old Nicky Sarames is shown at public school, where he has been successfully mainstreamed, interacting with friends and teachers. This warm and believable documentary emphasizes the ways in which he is like, not unlike, other children.

98 NIKKOLINA. Cineflics Ltd. 1978. 28 min. 16mm: $450 (EE681). Video: $300 (EE681). Rental: $45. Learning Corporation of America. (I-J).
Nikkolina wants most of all to ice skate, but when her great-aunt Sofia comes from Greece for a family wedding, scheduled the same day as a skating competition, Nikki must consider family loyalties and make a difficult decision.

99 NORTH AMERICAN INDIAN LEGENDS. Sal Bruno. 1973. 21 min. 16mm: $435 (71020). Video: $275 (71020). Rental: $65. BFA Educational Media. (I-J).
This attractive live-action film combines a romantic and compelling story of a maiden who married the Morning Star and then lost him forever, with a story of a young brave who brought corn to his people.

100 ONE. Mark Tarnawsky and Robert Just. 1980. 14 min. 16mm: $290. Video: $290. Rental: $30. Little Red Filmhouse. (Pr-P).
A lonely boy strolling through Central Park is drawn to the balloon stand. He can't afford the vendor's fee, but he encounters a mime who sparks his imagination by inflating an invisible balloon.

101 ONLY THE BALL WAS WHITE. WTTW. 1980. 16mm: $495 (426-0010). Video: 3/4": $198 (426-6010); 1/2": $129 (426-9010). Rental: $55. Films, Inc. (I-J).
With Paul Winfield narrating, photographic flashbacks and per-

sonal interviews capture the bittersweet era of the Negro Baseball League from its inception to its demise.

102 OVERTURE: LINH FROM VIETNAM. Learning Corporation of America. 1980. 26 min. 16mm: $450 (EP071). Video: $300 (EP071). Rental: $45. Learning Corporation of America. (J).
The friendship between a Vietnamese girl and a Mexican-American boy, begun through their mutual love of music, is threatened by the hostility of family and friends.

103 OWL WHO MARRIED A GOOSE. National Film Board of Canada. 1976. 7:30 min. 16mm: $170. Video: $120. Rental: $40. Churchill Films. (I-J).
With remarkable brown and white sand animation and minimal Eskimo dialogue, this legend of the owl who chooses a goose as its mate is a moving story of the problems of incompatible love. The owl's determination to live as the goose does leads to its death.

104 PADDINGTON AND THE "FINISHING TOUCH." Graham Clutterbuck. 1980. 5:30 min. 16mm: $210. Video: $210. Rental: $20. FilmFair Communications. (P-I).
Paddington, humorously adventurous as always, perilously trundles home a stone ball (the "finishing touch") for Mr. Brown's garden in this lively pastel-colored animated film. The distinctively British flavored tale is available on the two-episode reel Paddington and the "Finishing Touch"/Paddington and the Mystery Box.

105 PATRICK. Morton Schindel. 1973. 7 min. 16mm: $175 (MP145). Video: $90 (MP145VC). Rental: $20/day. Weston Woods. (Pr-P).
In a joyous, animated, non-narrated film based on the book by Quentin Blake (Walck, 1968), fish fly through the air, cows dance and become multi-colored, sweets grow on trees--all because of the enchanting music of an old violin.

106 PIGBIRD. National Film Board of Canada. 1983. 3 min. 16mm: $150. Video: $150. Rental: $30. National Film Board of Canada. (P-I-J).
The Canadian Customs Office presents a hilarious, animated message about what happens when a mysterious pigbird is smuggled into the country.

107 THE PLANT. National Film Board of Canada. 1983. 13 min. 16mm: $290. Video: $130. Rental: $29. Lucerne Films. (I-J).

Stop-action photography and special sound effects are used in this funny and suspenseful wordless film about a plant that takes over the home of a lovelorn young man.

108 PLASTIPHOBIA. 1973. 10 min. 16mm: $200. Rental: $30. International Film Foundation. (Pr-P-I-J).
This non-narrated clay animation film strings together such bizarre and improbable sights as dancing clay hands, a lion tamer who loses his head in the lion's mouth, a circus knife thrower who can't aim, and grotesque little clay men who knock each other about and into pieces.

109 PLEASE TAKE CARE OF YOUR TEETH. Nutshell Productions. 1983. 10 min. 16mm: $225 (1238). Video: $225 (1238). Rental: $45. Pyramid Film & Video. (P-I-J).
With wit and humor, this lively film presents the well-known basics of good oral hygiene in unusual ways.

110 RAG TAG CHAMPS. Roger Chenault. 1978. 48 min. 16mm: $615 (AC91). Video: $555 (AC91). Rental: $80. MTI Teleprograms, Inc. (P-I-J).
This is the story of plucky Jake, captain of his Little League team, who, threatened with being sent to a foster home, must win the right to stay with his Uncle Lenny. Based on the book _Jake_ by Alfred Slote (Lippincott, 1971), it is also the story of his baseball team's fight for survival.

111 REALLY ROSIE. Sheldon Riss. 1976. 26 min. 16mm: $475 (MP424). Video (both VHS and Beta): $50 (MPV424). Rental: $20/day. Weston Woods. (Pr-P).
Maurice Sendak's _Nutshell Library_ (Harper, 1962) characters are brought to life in a show starring Rosie of "Rosie's Door" fame. The catchy clever songs written and sung by Carole King and the lively, expressive animation make this film a sheer delight.

112 RED BALL EXPRESS. Perspective Films. 1975. 3 min. 16mm: $100 (3800). Video: $65 (3800). Rental: $30. Coronet Film & Video. (Pr-P-I-J).
By drawing on film, the filmmaker has created a spirited and imaginative visual adventure. Lively banjo music accentuates the everchanging images of wheels, tracks, and trains.

113 REVENGE OF THE NERD. Learning Corporation of America in association with Robert Keeshan Associates, Inc. 1983. 31 min. 16mm: $550 (EP181). Video: $450 (EP181). Rental: $55. Learning Corporation of America. (I-J).

Sick of being ridiculed, computer genius Bertram Cummings retaliates by appearing on his tormentors' television screens as the alien Non of Zonta.

114 ROOKIE OF THE YEAR. Daniel Wilson. 1975. 47 min. 16mm: $700 (F1917). Video: $200 (V1516). Rental: $70. Time-Life Video. (I-J).
When eleven-year-old Sharon Lee steps in as a substitute during Little League championship play-offs, she suffers frustration and confusion as the emotions of both children and adults are vented against her.

115 A ROUND FEELING. Kathleen Laughlin. 1974. 5 min. Eccentric Circle Cinema Workshop. (P-I-J). Availability unknown.
Images of a ferris wheel create whirling semi-abstract patterns in changing colors to the accompaniment of carnival music.

116 ROUNDABOUT. Churchill Films. 1978. 19 min. 16mm: $355. Video: $250. Rental: $40. Churchill Films. (P-I).
This is a sensitive fantasy in which a young boy and an elderly man share the magic of a toy carousel and what happens when the toy is stolen by the boy's friends.

117 SAMI HERDERS. National Film Board of Canada. 1979. 28 min. 16mm: $520. Video: $520. Rental: $55. Benchmark Films. (I-J).
This well-paced documentary shows the life-style of a family of Sami (Lapp) herders as they lead their reindeer across the frozen lands of northern Norway.

118 THE SAND CASTLE (LE CHATEAU DE SABLE). National film Board of Canada. 1977. 13 min. 16mm: $350. Video: $250. Rental: $40. National Film Board of Canada. (Pr-P-I-J).
A being of sand sculpts creatures to share its dune. Delightful in their diversity, these creatures build a sand castle and play upon it until a sandstorm threatens. The wordless film is done in three-dimensional sand animation.

119 SANDMAN. Eliot Noyes, Jr. 1973. 4 min. Eccentric Circle Cinema Workshop. (Pr-P). Availability unknown.
To the tune of lively fiddle music, this sand animation film presents rhythmically changing patterns with a walking figure, his pet dog, and a reappearing but easily vanquished monster.

120 SHOESHINE GIRL. Learning Corporation of America in association with Scholastic, Inc. 1980. 25 min. 16mm: $450 (EP001). Video: $300 (EP001). Rental: $45. Learning Corporation of America. (I-J).

Young Sarah spends the summer working at a shoeshine stand, learning the meaning of responsibility to herself as well as to others in this film based on Clyde Bulla's book (Harper, 1975).

121 THE SHOPPING BAG LADY. Learning Corporation of America. 1975. 21 min. 16mm: $425 (EE451). Video: $300 (EE451). Rental: $40. Learning Corporation of America. (I-J).

Set in Central Park, this exceptionally well-acted film tells the story of a homeless old woman and of a teenage girl's growing sensitivity to our society's cruelty to the elderly.

122 SKATEBOARD SAFETY. Pyramid. 1976. 13 min. 16mm: $325 (2908). Video: $325 (2908). Rental: $55. Pyramid Film & Video. (I-J).

A live-action film which concentrates more on "do" than "don't do" includes the stunts and competitions involved in the sport. The unusual camera angles and the variety in pacing make this an entertaining and instructive film on a popular subject.

123 THE SKATING RINK. Martin Tahse. 1975. 27 min. 16mm: $500 (EW453). Video: $350 (EW453). Rental: $50. Learning Corporation of America. (I-J).

Superior acting distinguishes this film based on the book by Mildred Lee (Seabury, 1969) in which a teenager who has difficulty in communicating learns to skate well and gains confidence in himself.

124 SNOW MONKEYS OF JAPAN. McGraw-Hill/RyersoL Ltd. 1975. 8 min. 16mm: $160 (4189). Video: $99.95 (4189). Rental: $25. AIMS Media. (I).

This is a fascinating glimpse of a band of monkeys who claim the hot springs of a river near Tokyo as their unusual habitat.

125 THE SNOWMAN. John Coates. 1982. 26 min. 16mm: $475 (MP288). Video (both VHS and Beta): $50. Rental: $40/day. Weston Woods. (P-I).

A young boy's snowman comes to life and they share a fantasy-filled adventure that extends from the front yard to the frozen North. Airy, dreamlike music and superb animation capture the joys of this special winter season. The film is based on Raymond Briggs's The Snowman (Random House, 1978).

126 THE SOAP BOX DERBY SCANDAL. Bob Cihi. 1975. 24 min. 16mm: $415 (MP422). Rental: $30/day. Weston Woods. (I-J).
The 1973 Soap Box Derby was marred by cheating on the part of the winner. This documentary powerfully depicts the long road to the finals as well as the ethical considerations of cheating.

127 THE SOUND COLLECTOR. National Film Board of Canada. 1982. 11:55 min. 16mm: $275 (106C182057). Video: $250 (116C0182057). Rental: $40. National Film Board of Canada. (P-I-J).
In an innovative and unique collage animation, two brothers transcend daily routines by collecting ordinary sounds and weaving them into a fantasy.

128 SOUND OF SUNSHINE, SOUND OF RAIN. Eda Godel Hallinan. 1983. 14:30 min. 16mm: $300. Video: $300. Rental: $30. FilmFair Communications. (P).
A blind boy enjoys abstract images of sound, color, and texture in this animated version of Florence Parry Heide's book (Parents Magazine Press, 1970).

129 SPACEBORNE. Lawrence Hall of Science, University of California at Berkeley. 1977. 14 min. 16mm: $325 (3078). Video: $325 (3078). Rental: $55. Pyramid Film & Video. (P-I-J).
The mission into space becomes a wondrous journey in this non-narrative documentary from NASA archives. The film is a montage of well-edited, non-simulated footage accompanied by resounding music.

130 SPLIT CHERRY TREE. 1982. 26 min. 16mm: $550 (EP131). Video: $425 (EP131). Rental: $55. Learning Corporation of America. (I-J).
Jesse Stuart's powerful and eloquent story of life in rural, depression-era Kentucky is artfully interpreted in this film. Its themes of peer pressure, family loyalty, and mutual respect are enhanced by the excellent photography.

131 STORM BOY. South Australia Film Commission. 1980. 30 min. 16mm: $500 (EP052). Video: $350 (EP052). Rental: $50. Learning Corporation of America. (I-J).
Set in a remote Australian wildlife sanctuary, this adaptation of Colin Thiele's book (Harper, 1978) depicts the relationships of nature-loving Storm Boy, his pet pelican, his father, and an aborigine friend.

132 A STORY, A STORY. Morton Schindel. 1973. 10 min. 16mm: $235 (MP123). Video (both VHS anL Leta): $50. Rental: $20/day. Weston Woods. (Pr-P).
This is the tale of how, long ago, Anansi the Spider paid the price to buy the sky god's stories when there were none on earth for children to hear. Vibrant colors and skillful animation recreate the Caldecott Medal Book by Gail Haley (Atheneum, 1970).

133 THE STORY OF CHRISTMAS. National Film Board of Canada. 1974. 8 min. Films, Inc. (P-I-J). No longer available.
Animated paper cutouts and Elizabethan music re-create the Christmas story. Stylized snowflakes fall and the brilliant star shines, enhancing the mystical quality of the event.

134 THE STREET. National Film Board of Canada. 1976. 10 min. 16mm: $275. Video: $250. Rental: $40. National Film Board of Canada. (J).
Imaginatively and lovingly animated, this provocative, thoughtful film focuses on the final years and death of a young boy's grandmother, depicting the ambiguity of the situation and his feelings. The film is based on Mordecai Richler's novel (New Republic, 1975).

135 THE STREET OF THE FLOWER BOXES. David Tapper and Suzette Tapper. 1973. 48 min. Films, Inc. (P-I-J). No longer available.
Carlos's involvement in creating and selling window boxes to the people of his block--one of the worst in New York City--helps create a sense of community in his neighborhood. This live-action film is based on the book by Peggy Mann (Coward, 1966).

136 A SWAMP ECOSYSTEM. National Geographic Society. 1983. 23 min. 16mm: $400 (05446). Video: $330 (05447). National Geographic Society. (I-J).
The fascinating land and waterways of the Okefenokee Swamp and the interrelationships among its plants and animals are explored through splendid nature photography.

137 THE SWINEHERD. Paul Hammerich. 1974. 13 min. 16mm: $275 (MP186). Video (both VHS and Beta): $50 (MPV186). Rental: $25/day. Weston Woods. (P-I).
A spoiled princess scorns the love of an honorable prince, but is willing to kiss a swineherd a hundred times for a silly musical toy, not realizing that the swineherd is actually the prince in disguise.

138 TALEB AND HIS LAMB. Ami Amitai. 1975. 16 min. 16mm: $345 (A176). Video: $345 (A176). Rental: $34.50. Barr Films. (I-J).
Taleb, a Bedouin boy, runs away with his lamb when his father insists that it be sold. The open-ended story conveys a good picture of Bedouin life while maintaining a universal appeal.

139 TANGRAM. Alan Slasor. 1975. 3 min. 16mm: $110 (3141). Video: $110 (3141). Rental: $45. Pyramid Film & Video. (Pr-P-I-J).
Seven geometric pieces of an ancient Chinese puzzle perform a ballet to baroque music. Inviting audience identification, the shapes rhythmically rearrange themselves to form various animals.

140 THE TAP DANCE KID. Learning Corporation of America. 1978. 33 min. 16mm: $500 (EE484). Video: $350 (EE484). Rental: $50. Learning Corporation of America. (I-J).
Twelve-year-old Emma and eight-year-old Willie challenge their middle-class parents' wishes when they fight for Willie's right to be a tap dancer. The film is based on the book Nobody's Family Is Going to Change by Louise Fitzhugh (Farrar, 1974).

141 TCHOU-TCHOU. National Film Board of Canada. 1973. 15 min. 16mm: $250 (3336). Video: $200; 12" VHS (XO3336); 1/2" Beta (WO3336); 3/4" U-Matic (VO3336). Rental: $25. Encyclopaedia Britannica Educational Corporation. (P-I-J).
Two children romp through their world and tame a fierce dragon. The building block figures are animated with incredible expression and agility; harmonica music heightens the suspenseful, playful elements of the story.

142 TEACH ME TO DANCE. National Film Board of Canada. 1979. 28 min. 16mm: $480 (101-0084). Video: 3/4": $198 (101-6084); 1/2": $129 (101-7084). Rental: $55. Films, Inc. (I-J).
Anti-Ukrainian prejudice jeopardizes the friendship between two girls living in Alberta in the early part of this century.

143 TEENY-TINY AND THE WITCH WOMAN. Morton Schindel. 1980. 14 min. 16mm: $275 (MP254). Video (both VHS and Beta): $50 (MPV254). Rental: $25/day. Weston Woods. (P-I).
Clever Teeny-Tiny and his two brothers escape the sinister witch woman in this Turkish folktale retold by Barbara Walker

(Pantheon, 1975). Michael Foreman's humorous illustrations are enhanced by atmospheric visual and aural effects and regional music.

144 THANK YOU, MA'M. Andrew Sugarman. 1976. 12 min. 16mm: $250 (21211). Video: $160 (21211). Rental: $25. Phoenix Film & Video. (I-J).
Seeing an older woman walking alone from work, a young boy tries to snatch her purse. Instead, the woman takes him home, feeds him, explains her outrage, and shows her understanding. The film is based on a short story by Langston Hughes.

145 TO TRY AGAIN ... AND SUCCEED! Bosustow Productions. 1979. 7:30 min. 16mm: $225. Video: $160. Rental: $40. Churchill Films. (P-I-J).
Distinctive ink and paint animation achieves a richly satisfying film, narrated by Orson Welles, stressing the universal, yet often frightening need to extend one's world, telling the story of an eaglet who fears to fly.

146 THE UGLY LITTLE BOY. Highgate Productions. 1977. 26 min. 16mm: $475 (EG576). Video: $350 (EG576). Rental: $40. Learning Corporation of America. (I-J).
A frightened Neanderthal boy is transported from the past for scientific investigation. The relationship between the boy and the project nurse leads to a harrowing climax in this provocative science fiction film, based on a short story by Isaac Asimov.

147 UP. Mike Hoover and Timothy Huntley. 1984. 14 min. 16mm: $350 (1115). Video: $350 (1115). Pyramid Film & Video. (I-J).
A young hang glider soars over stunning Western vistas in a symbolic story of his quest to fly like the eagle he has raised and set free.

148 VERONICA. National Film Board of Canada. 1978. 14 min. 16mm: $280. Video: $140. Rental: $18. The Media Guild. (P-I).
A warm documentary portrays the life of Veronica Nakarewicz, a first-generation Polish-Canadian child who lives above her parents' bakery on Queen Street in Toronto.

149 WHAT ENERGY MEANS. National Geographic Society. 1982. 15 min. 16mm: $280 (05385). Video: $240 (09386). Rental: $20. National Geographic Society. (I).
Utilizing ordinary household objects, Josh and his sister investi-

gate the interrelationships of the many forms of energy through firsthand experiences. A spirit of inquiry is conveyed through the creative treatment of the concepts.

150 WHAT MARY JO SHARED. Bernard Wilets. 1981. 13 min. 16mm: $275 (71957). Video: $175 (71957). Rental: $40. Phoenix Film & Video. (Pr-P).

The warm story of shy Mary Jo, who searches for something "special" to share with her young classmates, is portrayed in a live-action film based on the book by Janice Udry (Whitman, 1966).

151 WHERE IS DEAD? Life Style Productions. 1975. 19 min. 16mm: $345 (3417). Video: $275 (VC3417). Rental: $34.50. Encyclopaedia Britannica Educational Corporation. (I-J).

In approaching an understanding of the death of her older brother, a six-year-old girl learns from her parents and friends how memory and feeling bring into perspective the hurt and frustration of loss.

152 WHERE THE WILD THINGS ARE. Morton Schindel. 1973. 8 min. 16mm: $195 (MP84). Video (both VHS and Beta): $50 (MP84VC). Rental: $20/day. Weston Woods. (Pr-P).

Sent to bed without supper, Max sails into a forest of wild creatures. Unusual animation gives the wild things a hazy, dreamlike quality, and an inventive soundtrack uses catcalls, foot-stomping, band music, and other elements to present the Maurice Sendak story, a Caldecott Medal Book (Harper, 1963) in a new and compelling way.

153 WILD GREEN THINGS IN THE CITY. Geode. 1974. 11 min. 16mm: $230. Video: 3/4": $198; 1/2": $142. Rental: $40. Films, Inc. (P-I-J).

A young girl finds wildflowers in vacant lots and between cracks in the sidewalk and then creates her own rooftop garden in this non-narrated extension of the book by Anne Ophelia Dowden (Crowell, 1972).

154 WIND. 1973. 10 min. 16mm: $150 (LEF631). Video: $75 (LEF631). Rental: $25. Learning Corporation of America. (P).

A small child, giggling and playing in the wind, is surrounded by swirling colors and images of houses, horses, and kites flying past in this unusual and handsomely illustrated animated film.

155 WIZARD OF SPEED AND TIME. Mike Jittlov. 1979. 3 min. Pyramid Film & Video. (Pr-P-I-J). No longer available.
The Wizard whizzes to Hollywood and whirls through a film studio in this energizing, pixilated high.

156 THE WONDERFUL LOLLYPOP ROOSTER. 1973. 8 min. 16mm: $200. Video: $120. Sterling Educational Films. (Pr-P).
A magic lollypop from a mysterious stranger carries a little boy into a series of dreamlike adventures in this animated, non-narrated film.

157 ZEA. National Film Board of Canada. 1982. 5 min. 16mm: $150 (106-0081-022). Video: $150 (116-0081-022). Rental: $35. National Film Board of Canada. (P-I-J).
Sophisticated technology and high-speed photography capture an unknown entity as it moves and changes to the vibrant strains of Vaughan Williams's "Fantasia on a Theme by Thomas Tallis." Viewers are held spellbound as the drama unfolds to its delightful, unexpected conclusion.

158 ZLATEH THE GOAT. Morton Schindel. 1973. 20 min. 16mm: $375 (MP419). Video (both VHS and Beta): $50 (MP419VC). Rental: $50. Weston Woods. (I-J).
This live-action film, based on the Newbery Honor Book by Isaac Bashevis Singer (Harper, 1966), tells of a little boy lost in a snowstorm on his way to market to sell the family's beloved goat.

159 A ZOO'S EYE VIEW: DAWN TO DARK. Milan Herzog. 1973. 11 min. 16mm: $225 (3180). Video: $225; 1/2" VHS (XO3180); 1/2" Beta II (WO3180); 3/4" U-Matic (VO3180). Rental: $22.50. Encyclopaedia Britannica Educational Corporation. (Pr-P-I).
Intriguing glimpses of the activity of a day at the zoo highlight this non-narrative film.

Notable Filmstrips

1 ANCIENT MONUMENTS AND MYSTERIES. National Geographic Society. 1978. (03995). 1 fs, 46 fr. with cassette. 14 min. $31.95. National Geographic Society. (I-J).

The origins, purposes, and creation of cave paintings, stone edifices, monumental structures, and enigmatic figures discovered at various sites in Europe, Asia, Africa, and the Americas are briefly suggested in this introductory survey of ancient art and architecture. Dramatic color photos visually expand the narration and arouse interest in further research.

2 BABAR THE KING. Spectra Films. 1977. (394-07536-6). 2 fs, 131 fr./102 fr. with 2 cassettes. 9:59 min./8:34 min. $48.75 Random House. (P).

This filmstrip, based on the book by Jean de Brunhoff (Random House, 1937), is a captivating blend of visuals and sound that reveals the details of de Brunhoff's vibrant illustrations while giving vivacity to the king, his subjects, and the happenings in Celesteville.

3 BEN'S TRUMPET. Random House. 1980. (394-66059-5). 1 fs, 110 fr. with cassette. 11:08 min. $27.50. Random House. (P-I-J).

Ben dreams of being able to play the trumpet as well as the man from the Zig Zag Club can. The combination of vibrant color, snappy pacing, and an original jazz score adds a totally new dimension to the Caldecott Honor Book by Rachel Isadora (Greenwillow, 1979).

4 THE BERENSTAIN BEARS AND THE SPOOKY OLD TREE. Paratore Pictures. 1978. (394-00933-9). 1 fs, 56 fr. with cassette. 6 min. $25. Random House. (P).

Just the right amount of eerie background music, dramatic narration, and spooky pictures enhance this delightfully scary story by Stan and Jan Berenstain (Random House, 1978).

5 THE CAMERA OF MY FAMILY: FOUR GENERATIONS IN GERMANY. Anti-Defamation League of B'nai B'rith. 1979. (HVS-627). 1 fs, 123 fr. with cassette. 18 min. $40. Anti-Defamation League of B'nai B'rith. (J).
This filmstrip, based on the book by Catherine Hanf Noren (Knopf, 1976), adapted by Milton Meltzer, is a thought-provoking, well-planned documentary that uses family photographs to illustrate and personalize the plight of Jews before and during World War II.

6 A CHAIR FOR MY MOTHER. Random House-Miller-Brody. 1983. (676-30680-2). 1 fs, 81 fr. with cassette. 8 min. $27.50. Random House. (Pr-P).
After a young girl, her mother, and her grandmother lose everything in an apartment fire, they save coins in a huge jar to buy a new easy chair. The realistic sounds of urban life and vivid watercolor paintings support the child narrator's enthusiastic account, adding a new dimension to the Caldecott Honor Book by Vera B. Williams (Greenwillow, 1982).

7 CHINA: A CULTURAL HERITAGE. From the series China: The Land and the People. January Productions. 1979. (JPC 1028). 1 fs, 66 fr. with cassette. 18 min. $24. (Series with 4 fs/4 cassettes is $92.) January Productions. (I-J).
Stills of paintings, calligraphy, musical instruments, crafts, and scrolls trace the evolution of Chinese philosophy and art from ancient uses to an integration of traditional and contemporary life.

8 THE CITY. Clearvue, Inc. 1978. (CL 360-C). 6 fs, av. 45 fr. ea. with 6 cassettes. 8 min. ea. Teacher's guide. $126. Clearvue, Inc. (I-J).
Concepts of community pride, responsibility, and interdependency are thoughtfully explored as striking color photographs show governmental, cultural, and financial institutions, skyscrapers, neighborhoods, and occupational and recreational opportunities. Unusual camera angles and a lively jazz/blues score create a montage of places and people that convey a sense of the vitality and excitement of city life.

9 THE CLOWN OF GOD. Weston Woods. 1980. (SF 260C). 1 fs, 53 fr. with cassette. 15 min. $22. Weston Woods. (Pr-P).

Renaissance music enhances the tender story of Giovanni, whose last act in life is to juggle his colored balls as a gift for the Madonna and Child. The narrator's mellow tone complements the softness of the illustrations from Tomie dePaola's book (Harcourt, 1978).

10 COLOMBIA: A WAY OF LIFE. Troll Associates. 1978. (SC 119). 2 fs, av. 64 fr. with 2 cassettes. 8 min. $44. Troll Associates. (I-J).
Urban life is contrasted with rural life through an examination of two families with emphasis on art, food, dress, schooling, modes of transportation, celebrations, and environment. Colorful photographs and easy-flowing narration create a vital, appealing portrait of this South American country and its people.

11 A DARK DARK TALE. Weston Woods. 1982. (SF 275-C). 1 fs, 27 fr. with cassette. 5 min. $22. Weston Woods. (Pr-P).
The black cat stalks away from the dark, dark moor into the eerie mansion, down the long hall, to a mysterious cupboard. Richly detailed illustrations, haunting music, and the narrator's spooky voice enhance the suspenseful mood of this dramatic interpretation of Ruth Brown's book (Dial, 1981).

12 DAVID AND DOG. Weston Woods. 1979. (SF 244C). 1 fs, 43 fr. with cassette. 8 min. $22. Weston Woods. (Pr-P).
Clear, distinctive, contemporary illustrations that reflect warmth, a light instrumental background that sets the mood, and expressive narration bring to life Shirley Hughes's tender story (Prentice-Hall, 1978) of young David, who misplaces his toy dog and becomes inconsolable.

13 DEAR MR. HENSHAW. Random House. 1985. (676-31095-8). 2 fs, 180 fr. with 2 cassettes. 40:06 min. $52. Random House. (I).
This exceptional dramatization, based on the Newbery award-winning novel by Beverly Cleary (Morrow, 1983), is a two-part filmstrip telling the story of Leigh Botts, his correspondence with his favorite author, and his subsequent growth toward maturity. Original, live-action color photography and an out-standing soundtrack with unaffected dialogue blend to make this a noteworthy adaptation.

14 DOCTOR DESOTO. Weston Woods. 1983. (SF 284C). 1 fs, 47 fr. with cassette. 9 min. $22. Weston Woods. (P).

The familiar sounds of a dentist's office, sprightly music, and droll British narration combine with William Steig's humorous art to create an irresistible filmstrip based on the Newbery Honor Book (Farrar, 1982) in which the mice couple outmaneuvers their ill-intentioned patient, the fox.

15 THE DOLL MAKER. Warner Educational Productions. 1978. (165). 4 fs, av. 86 fr. with 2 cassettes. 12 min. ea. $134.50. Warner Educational Productions. (J).
In brief, lucid steps accompanied by detailed photographs, the methods of creating art dolls, such as Kewpie, Jester, and Ballerina, are presented. From the making of molds to the sewing of costumes and from the casting of body parts to the inserting of eyes, techniques are precisely, minutely, and logically illustrated and described.

16 EARTH, AIR, AND WATER. From the series Grassroots Science, Set 4. Denoyer-Geppert Audiovisuals. 1979. (DG5-54050). 4 fs, av. 50 fr. ea. with 4 cassettes. 4:30 min. ea. $102. Charles Clark Company, Inc. (P-I).
Photographs of outstanding composition and clarity show young children exploring how moving water, the actions of wind, water evaporation, and the amount of annual rainfall determine the nature of plants and change the shape and condition of the land. The children question what they observe and seek explanations in dialogues with an adult narrator.

17 THE ELEPHANT'S CHILD. Spoken Arts, Inc. 1976. (SAC 2033 fs/cassette); (SA 203333 fs/record). 1 fs, 67 fr. with cassette or record. 17:45 min. $39.95. Spoken Arts, Inc. (P).
The endearing Kipling tale of the satiable little elephant is rendered faithfully and narrated dramatically with appropriate sound effects. Three-dimensional paper cutout visuals suit both the character and mood of this beloved Just So Story.

18 FABLES. Random House. 1981. (364-07703-2). 1 fs, 135 fr. with cassette. 18 min. $27.50. Random House. (P-I).
Seven fables from Arnold Lobel's Caldecott award-winning book (Harper, 1980) are presented in this engaging filmstrip. The unique flavor of each fable is augmented by original music ranging from Middle Eastern to American folk. Excellent vocal interpretation adds to the inventiveness of the dramatization.

19 FARMER PALMER'S WAGON RIDE. Miller-Brody. 1976. (394-76481-1). 2 fs, 47 fr./50 fr. with 2 cassettes. 7:51 min./8:12 min. $48.75. Random House. (P).

The comedy of William Steig's book (Farrar, 1974) is intensified through the skillful reproduction of his illustrations, low-key narration, and fitting background music, all of which combine to make this a memorable story of misadventure.

20 FOOLISH BARTEK. National Film Board of Canada. 1977. Donars Productions. (P-I). Availability unknown.

This silent filmstrip delicately captures the humor and verity of the traditional Polish tale of Bartek, who gains a series of magical gifts through his acts of kindness, but loses them all because of his foolishness. Tasteful layouts and colorfully simple but appropriate illustrations enhance the filmstrip, which requires no narration to achieve an imaginative air.

21 GEORGE WASHINGTON AND THE WHISKEY REBELLION: TESTING THE CONSTITUTION. Learning Corporation of America. 1978. 2 fs, ea. 125 fr. with cassette. 10 min. Learning Corporation of America. (I-J). No longer available.

Selected frames from the 16mm film (1975) of the same title are used to tell the story of the testing of the new Constitution by Pennsylvania farmers who violently opposed the tax on whiskey, forcing Washington to quell the rebellion to preserve the integrity of the constitution. Ample sound effects, dramatic narration, and well-paced visuals capture the excitement of the incident.

22 GILGAMESH AND THE MONSTER IN THE WOOD. Acorn Films, 1976. 1 fs with cassette. Acorn Films. (I-J). Availability unknown.

In a version of the epic of Gilgamesh, the episodes of the origin of Enkidu and the destruction of Humbaba are told with dramatic restraint. Mythological atmosphere is created by almost primitive drawings against a background of flowingly muted colors, which are reminiscent of Bernarda Bryson's illustrations in her book Gilgamesh, Man's First Story (Harper, 1967).

23 THE GOLEM. Weston Woods. 1979. (SF 248C). 1 fs, 60 fr. with cassette. 10 min. $22. Weston Woods. (P-I).

Rich, breathtaking artwork is effectively adapted from Beverly Brodsky McDermott's Caldecott Honor Book (Lippincott, 1976) to magnify the impact of this gripping Jewish legend. An introduction by the author-illustrator offers enlightening background information about the origin of the clay figure known as "the golem."

24 GRANT WOOD: HIS LIFE AND PAINTINGS. Rachel Stevenson. 1985. 4 fs, 73-79 fr. with 4 cassettes. 17 min. ea. $135. International Film Bureau, Inc. (I-J).
This production blends photographs of several of Grant Wood's works, interviews with persons who knew him, criticisms about his paintings, and photographs of the Wood family and friends. The viewer learns about Grant Wood's life and paintings, his family, friends, teachers, early school experiences, and his first attempts at painting.

25 GRASSROOTS SCIENCE; SETS 1, 2, AND 3. Denoyer-Geppert Audiovisuals. 1978. (Set 1: DG5-54000); (Set 2: DG5-54010); (Set 3: DG5-54020). 12 fs, av. 55 fr. with 12 cassettes. 6 min. ea. $102 per set. Charles Clark Company, Inc. (P-I).
Child-appealing early science lessons in this uniformly high-quality series incorporate the learning skills of observation, comparison, and questioning. Superior photography, excellent scripts, and lively original scores are blended in captivating educational experiences.

26 THE GREY LADY AND THE STRAWBERRY SNATCHER. Random House. 1981. (394-07709-1). 1 fs, 109 fr. with cassette. 10 min. $27.50. Random House. (P).
Molly Bang's Caldecott Honor wordless picture book (Four Winds, 1980) is interpreted through the use of artistic camera angles, quick pacing, and lush color. An original musical score effectively heightens the sense of suspense as the strawberry snatcher pursues the grey lady from marketplace to home.

27 HARRY BY THE SEA. Miller-Brody, 1977. (394-64536-7). 1 fs, 73 fr. with cassette. 10:14 min. $25. Random House. (P).
This faithful adaptation of Gene Zion's book (Harper, 1965) expands Margaret Graham's humorous drawings and Harry's predicaments through varied visual perspectives and animated narrative accompanied by delightful music and suitable sound effects.

28 HENRY THE EXPLORER. Weston Woods. 1977. (SF 196C). 1 fs, 37 fr. with cassette. 6 min. $22. Weston Woods. (P).
Based on the charming story written by Mark Taylor and illu-

strated by Graham Booth (Atheneum, 1966), the filmstrip adaptation enhances Henry and Angus's adventure with good narration, atmospheric sound effects, and lively musical accompaniment.

29 HORTON HATCHES THE EGG. Random House. 1976. (676-30944-5). 2 fs, 43 fr./72 fr. with 2 cassettes. 6 min./8 min. $48.75. Random House. (P).
Dr. Seuss's popular egg-sitting story (Random House, 1940) is dramatized by a comic balance of voices and projected with adroitly paced colored picture sequences.

30 HOW DO FAMILIES CHANGE? From the My Family and Me series. Encyclopaedia Britannica Educational Corporation. 1981. (242299K). 1 fs, 47 fr. with cassette. 5:16 min. $35. (Series set of 4 fs/4 cassettes is $126.) Encyclopaedia Britannica Educational Corporation. (P-I).
Realistic photographs with a gentle, supportive narration show how family members in a number of different cultures are sustained by each other's loving concern through times of change.

31 THE HUNDRED PENNY BOX. Miller-Brody. 1979. (394-76914-7). 2 fs, av. 100 fr. with 2 cassettes. 24 min. ea. $52. Random House. (I-J).
A touching story of love and aging is portrayed in realistic, yellow-and-green-tone mood photographs with sensitive narration. Based on Sharon Bell Mathis's Newbery Honor Book (Viking, 1975), the filmstrip focuses on family relationships and feelings.

32 THE ICE CREAM FACTORY/MAKING BREAD. From The Weaver, the Baker, the Bicycle Maker series. Denoyer-Geppert Audiovisuals. 1979. (Set: DG5-69500). 6 fs, av. 65 fr. ea. with 6 cassettes. 7 min. ea. $148 for set. Charles Clark Company, Inc. (P-I).
Two exceptional filmstrips from this high-quality set use color photographs, a lively script, and bright music to follow the manufacture of ice cream and bread from raw materials to finished product. Each step of the process is carefully explained while maintaining the excitement of watching the product evolve.

33 JOURNEY TO MOSKA. From Stories Told by Native Americans series. Crocus Productions. 1977. (13818-23818K). 1 fs, 67 fr. with cassette. 10 min. $37. Encyclopaedia Britannica Educational Corporation. (I-J).
A Hopi tale of a young man's struggle to accept both the spirit

world and the earthly world is effectively presented with detailed doll figures, realistic settings, and dramatic visuals.

34 THE LEGEND OF THE BLUEBONNET: AN OLD TALE OF TEXAS. Listening Library, Inc. 1983. (GSF 703). 1 fs, 45 fr. with cassette. 9 min. $24.95. Listening Library, Inc. (P-I).

An Indian child sacrifices her most prized possession--a warrior doll--to save the Comanche people. The sign of the Great Spirit's acceptance of her gift is rain and fields of bluebonnets. A Native American mood is created by rhythmic flute music and the vibrant, stylized illustrations from Tomie dePaola's book (Putnam, 1983).

35 A LIKELY STORY. Encyclopaedia Britannica Educational Corporation. 1978. (17049K). 4 fs, av. 71 fr. ea. with cassette. Av. 5 min. ea. $126. Encyclopaedia Britannica Educational Corporation. (P-I).

The imaginative stories in this series succeed in their design to stimulate interest in reading and numerous other related language arts activities. Versatility of use is provided by a thoughtful guide, by captions along with sound, and by varying the illustrative technique between cartoon drawings and photographs.

36 THE LOCH NESS MONSTER & THE ABOMINABLE SNOWMAN; ATLANTIS & UFOs. From Mysteries Old and New set. National Geographic Society. 1982. (04457). 2 fs, av. 53 fr. ea. with 2 cassettes. Av. 19 min. ea. $61.95. National Geographic Society. (I-J).

Well-known popular and mysterious phenomena are objectively presented through vivid photographs, artists' renderings, and a thought-provoking narrative. The filmstrips, which can also be viewed separately, can help expand children's understanding of the processes involved in scientific inquiry.

37 MEET THE NEWBERY AUTHOR: ARNOLD LOBEL. Miller-Brody. 1978. (394-77255-5). 1 fs, 97 fr. with cassette. 10 min. $37.50. Random House. (P-I).

Informal photos, family stills, and many samples from Lobel's books complement information about the author/illustrator's working methods in a lively fashion.

38 MEET THE NEWBERY AUTHOR: VIRGINIA HAMILTON. Miller-Brody. 1976. 1 fs, 101 fr. with cassette or record. (394-77249-0 fs/cassette); (394-77232-6 fs/record). 15 min. $37.50. Random House. (I-J).

Old family snapshots, stills of Hamilton and her family at home, and enactments of scenes from M. C. Higgins the Great are blended with conversation and narration to present an intimate picture of the noted author.

39 MERRY EVER AFTER: THE STORY OF TWO MEDIEVAL WEDDINGS. Viking. 1977. (0-670-90566-6). 1 fs, 70 fr. with cassette. 18:09 min. $23.95. Live Oak Media. (P-I).

The rich details of Joe Lasker's illustrations from his book (Viking, 1976) are adroitly framed to augment the contrast and similarities of the customs and people of medieval Europe. Vivid narration and contemporary music combine to create a work for aesthetic pleasure and historical enlightenment.

40 MORRIS'S DISAPPEARING BAG. Weston Woods. 1978. (SF 230C). 1 fs, 38 fr. with cassette. 6 min. $22. Weston Woods. (Pr-P).

The tale of Morris's one-upmanship with his brother and sisters on Christmas is one of Rosemary Wells's most successful and charming books (Dial, 1975). This filmstrip version, narrated with well-paced clarity and humor, provides a format which enables large-group enjoyment of a tiny holiday gem.

41 MUSHROOM IN THE RAIN. Macmillan Library Services. 1976. 1 fs with cassette or record. Macmillan Library Services. (P). Availability unknown.

The dynamic pacing of the visuals combines smoothly with a piano accompaniment that evokes the struggling and squishing of the animals under the mushroom. Gentle narration effectively expresses the whimsical nature of the story, which is based on the book by Mirra Ginsburg, illustrated by Jose Aruego and Ariane Dewey (Macmillan, 1974).

42 NIGHTGOWN OF THE SULLEN MOON. Random House. 1985. (537-69401-3). 1 fs, 47 fr. with cassette. 7:20 min. $26. Random House. (I).

Zoe Caldwell narrates Nancy Willard's fantasy (Harcourt, 1983) about the sullen moon. Longing for a nightgown for her "billionth birthnight," the moon finds a splendid gown of the softest blue flannel flecked with stars. David McPhail's watercolors enhance the mood of the story, while Arthur Custer's musical score evokes the otherworldliness of the universe and differentiates between the episodes set in the heavens and those on earth.

43 NO ROSES FOR HARRY. Miller-Brody. 1977. (394-64542-1). 1 fs, 69 fr. with cassette. 9 min. $25. Random House. (P).
This faithful adaptation of Gene Zion's book (Harper, 1958) expands Margaret Graham's humorous drawings and Harry's predicaments through varied visual perspectives and animated narrative accompanied by delightful music and suitable sound effects.

44 NO SCHOOL TODAY. Macmillan Library Services. 1976. 1 fs with cassette or record. Macmillan Library Services. (P). Availability unknown.
Spunky ragtime background and touches of sound effects blend with colorful visuals in a nicely paced filmstrip that captures and enlivens the characters of Elizabeth and Edward and the nuances of their contemporary cat community. The filmstrip is based on the book by Franz Brandenberg, illustrated by Aliki (Macmillan, 1975).

45 NOAH'S ARK. Weston Woods. 1978. (SF 237C). 1 fs, 67 fr. with cassette. 11 min. $22. Weston Woods. (Pr-P).
Peter Spier's Caldecott Medal account (Doubleday, 1977) of Noah's ark is enriched by focusing on vital details from his intricate drawings, and even more by adding all the realistic background sounds and animal noises which might have accompanied the guests aboard this famous ship.

46 THE OLD WOMAN OF THE MOUNTAIN. Coronet. 1976. 1 fs with cassette or record. Coronet. (P). No longer available.
To save the village below from destruction, Akazibanba survives the dangerous climb up the mountain to bring rice cakes to the Giant Baby and to serve the old woman of the mountain. Strikingly unusual sets with finely detailed puppets artfully depict the excitement of the Japanese legend.

47 ONCE A MOUSE. Miller-Brody. 1977. (394-76473-0). 1 fs, 42 fr. with cassette. 6 min. $27.50. Random House. (P).
Based on Marcia Brown's Caldecott Medal Book (Scribner, 1961), this filmstrip adaptation skillfully constructs and frames the original woodcuts to focus on the action as it evolves. Arthur Custer's original score sets a magical mood that hints at the Indian origin of the fable.

48 THE OWL AND THE LEMMING (AN ESKIMO LEGEND). Donars Productions. 1976. 1 fs with cassette. Donars Productions. (P-I). Availability unknown.
An owl's vanity causes him to lose his prey in a familiar fable set in the Arctic tundra. Authentic Eskimo voices and songs animate the sealskin characters in frames taken directly from the original 16mm film.

49 PERSPECTIVE DRAWING. Educational Dimensions. 1978. (671). 2 fs, av. 80 fr. ea. with 2 cassettes. Av. 16 min. ea. $77. Educational Dimensions. (I-J).
The definition of perspective and how to use and draw it correctly are well explained, as the works of Wyeth, Estes, Dali, and others provide many examples of both one-point and two-point perspective.

50 THE PLANET OF JUNIOR BROWN. Miller-Brody. 1977. (394-77086-2). 2 fs, 127 fr./123 fr. with 2 cassettes. 19:58 min./19:05 min. $52. Random House. (J).
An unusual adaptation of a serious novel, Virginia Hamilton's Newbery Honor Book (Macmillan, 1971), this filmstrip features skillful editing, narration, dialogue, and illustration in an excellent presentation of a haunting story of city life and a boy's descent into madness.

51 POETRY EXPLAINED BY KARLA KUSKIN. Weston Woods. 1980. (SF465). 1 fs, 43 fr. with cassette. 16 min. $33. Weston Woods. (I-J).
Interviews with the poet and readings coupled with her artwork make Kuskin and her work accessible in this fascinating and insightful production.

52 RAMONA THE PEST. From First Choice: Authors and Books program, Unit 9. Pied Piper Productions. 1977. 1 fs, 93 fr. with cassette. 11:12 min. (Plus interview cassette. 11:11 min.) $35. Pied Piper Productions. (P-I).
Capturing Ramona's entry into kindergarten, brief episodes are dramatized with children's voices and with illustrations directly reflecting those in Beverly Cleary's book (Morrow, 1968).

53 READING FOR THE FUN OF IT: REALISTIC FICTION. Guidance Associates. 1976. (02-70910). 1 fs, 89 fr. with cassette. 15 min. $47. Guidance Associates. (I).
Narrated sequences of real children portraying book characters reveal just enough plot to arouse acute reader curiosity. This

filmstrip is exceptional in scope, approach, quality of visuals, and persuasiveness.

54 RIDE THE COLD WIND. Westport Communications Group. 1976. (394-06342-6). 1 fs, 50 fr. with cassette. 10 min. $25. Random House. (P-I).
Bold Leonard Fisher woodcuts tell Anico Surany's story (Putnam, 1964) of a young Andean boy seeking to fulfill his dream of catching the great fish of Lake Titicaca. Enhanced by pipe music background, the story presents an authentic picture of Andean culture and the growth of one child.

55 ROSEY GRIER: BELIEVING IN YOURSELF. From The Courage to Be Me set. Pied Piper Productions. 1979. 1 fs, 201 fr. with cassette. 21 min. $39. Pied Piper Productions. (I-J).
Former Los Angeles Rams player Rosey Grier shares his struggles as he narrates this documentary that emphasizes his drive for self-growth and confidence while overcoming personal difficulties.

56 SEASONS OF POETRY. Society for Visual Education. 1976. (BJ445-SATC). 4 fs, av. 35 fr. ea. with 4 cassettes. Av. 8 min. ea. $127 or $35 for individual fs/cassette. Society for Visual Education. (I-J).
Brief, child-centered poems on the four seasons are lightly read and impressively illustrated with vivid nature photography. Introduced by effective music, the poems are given gentle continuity by the narrator, and visual interest is maintained by contrasting panoramic views with startling minutiae.

57 SHADOW. Weston Woods. 1983. (SF 282C). 1 fs, 33 fr. with cassette. 9 min. $22. Weston Woods. (P-I).
Marcia Brown sensitively narrates Blaise Cendrars's lyrical exploration of an entity called "Shadow." Accompanied by original music that underscores the eerie mood, this filmstrip illuminates the sophisticated concepts and artwork of the Caldecott Medal Book (Scribner, 1982).

58 SIMON'S BOOK. Random House. 1985. (537-69337-7). 1 fs, 63 fr. with cassette. 6:32 min. $26. Random House. (P).
A young boy's sketch of a big, furry beast and a character named Simon comes alive after the boy goes to bed. Henrik Drescher's (Lothrop, 1983) intense, frenetic, and contemporary drawings create a wild and amusing romp through the pages of the boy's sketchbook with the beast in hot pursuit of Simon,

two pens, and an ink bottle. A soundtrack with quiet, deliberate narration and synthesized music, which pulsates to a subtle reggae beat, echoes the humor and the vibrant mood of the magical illustrations.

59 THE SOLAR SYSTEM/BEYOND THE SOLAR SYSTEM. National Geographic Society. 1976. 2 fs, ea. 45 fr. with cassette. 13 min. ea. National Geographic Society. (I-J). No longer available.

Two timely presentations of our changing view of the universe investigate such topics as asteroids, meteors, comets, black holes, quasars, pulsars, galaxies, novas, the characteristics of stars, and radio telescopes in a manner that challenges the viewer to further study. Space odyssey-type music suggests mood without overwhelming this excellent survey of the universe.

60 A SPECIAL TRADE. From That's Delightful series. Encyclopaedia Britannica Educational Corporation. 1980. (24196K). 1 fs, 55 fr. with cassette. 6:51 min. $35. Encyclopaedia Britannica Educational Corporation. (Pr-P).

Simple line drawings and gentle narration underscored by a harmonica portray a feeling of concern as a small girl and an old man trade care and friendship with each other.

61 SPRING/SUMMER/FALL. From Life Times: The Seasons, Grassroots Science, Set 5. Denoyer-Geppert. 1979. (DG5-54060). 3 fs, av. 55 fr. ea. with 3 cassettes. Av. 23 min. ea. $102 for set of 4 fs/cassettes. Charles Clark Company, Inc. (P-I).

Unusually evocative and detailed photographs, sound effects, and a well-paced, child-centered narration in these three filmstrips invite the examination of physical and behavioral changes experienced by various species during the year.

62 STEVEN KELLOGG'S YANKEE DOODLE. Weston Woods. 1976. (SF 173C). 1 fs, 53 fr. with cassette. 10 min. $22. Weston Woods. (Pr-P).

The famous poem is narrated by a child whose enthusiasm and clarity seem to be just what author Edward Bangs had in mind. Kellogg's vivid illustrations from the book (Four Winds, 1976) are framed and repeated for optimum effect in humor and detail, and the chorus of children's voices that concludes the presentation offers an irresistible invitation to join in.

63 THE STONECUTTER. Weston Woods. 1976. (SF 178C). 1 fs, 33 fr. with cassette. 7 min. $22. Weston Woods. (P).

Tasaku wishes for more and more power, but he finds, too late, that as a stonecutter he is already perhaps the most powerful of all. Japanese music accompanying the bright collages of oriental motifs enriches the visual experience of Gerald McDermott's book (Viking, 1975).

64 STORY OF A BOOK SECOND EDITION: WITH MARGUERITE HENRY. From First Choice: Authors and Books series, Unit 19. Pied Piper Productions. 1982. (A-19). 1 fs, 124 fr. with cassette. 16 min. $35. Pied Piper Productions. (P-I).

Marguerite Henry discusses the creative process of researching, writing, illustrating, and producing one of her many books. Clear visuals and a candid narration combine to effectively introduce this well-known author and relate the many steps necessary for creating a book--from inception to readers' responses.

65 SUGARING TIME. Random House. 1985. (676-31071-0). 1 fs, 137 fr. with cassette. 22 min. $30. Random House. (I-J).

A Vermont family enterprise, tapping sap from trees and processing it into maple syrup, is factually and vividly recounted in this striking black-and-white photodocumentary. Authentic sound effects together with original flute and guitar music enhance this poetically descriptive narrative, based on the Newbery Honor Book by Kathryn Lasky (Macmillan, 1983), of an affectionate family cooperating, celebrating, and producing a delectable product.

66 SWEET WHISPERS, BROTHER RUSH. Random House/Miller-Brody. 1983. (676-30641-1). 2 fs, 147 fr./138 fr. with 2 cassettes. 20:57 min./18:29 min. $52. Random House. (I-J).

The ghost of Brother Rush appears to guide Tree as she struggles to comprehend the mysteries and secrets of the family's past and slowly realizes her brother Dab is critically ill. Evocative drawings enhance the measured cadence of Virginia Hamilton's narration, from her Newbery Honor Book (Philomel, 1982), to create a deeply moving portrayal of family life.

67 TELL-TALE HEART. From Middle Grades Showcase: Famous American Stories series. Encyclopaedia Britannica Educational Corporation. 1980. (24351K). 1 fs, 69 fr. with cassette. 11:15 min. $35. Encyclopaedia Britannica Educational Corporation. (I-J).
A fine blend of voice, sound effects, color, lighting, and timing perfectly convey the mood of horror and madness in Poe's short story, portrayed here with original illustrations.

68 TEN, NINE, EIGHT. Random House. 1985. (676-30949-6). 1 fs, 37 fr. with cassette. 4:17 min. $27.50. Random House. (Pr-P).
Father and daughter share in a lyrical lullaby as they count down to bedtime. Natural sound effects and soft synthesized music provide a soothing accompaniment to the brilliant pictures from Molly Bang's Caldecott Honor Book (Greenwillow, 1983).

69 THE TIGER SKIN RUG. From That's Delightful series. Encyclopaedia Britannica Educational Corporation. 1980. (24199K). 1 fs, 41 fr. with cassette. 6:25 min. $35. Encyclopaedia Britannica Educational Corporation. (Pr-P).
Authentic East Indian music and effective narration enhance the illustrations from Gerald Rose's humorous and fast-paced story (Prentice-Hall, 1979) of a jungle tiger who lives temporarily undetected as a rug in a rajah's palace.

70 THE TREASURE. Weston Woods. 1980. (SF 250C). 1 fs, 26 fr. with cassette. 6 min. $22. Weston Woods. (P-I).
Uri Shulevitz's tale, a Caldecott Honor Book (Farrar, 1978), of journeying far to find what is near is gracefully told, artfully visualized, and memorably accompanied by the expressive strains of "The Moldau."

71 TREASURE OF THE BOY KING TUT. Educational Dimensions. 1978. (116). 2 fs, av. 50 fr. with 2 cassettes. Av. 12 min. ea. $50. Educational Dimensions. (P-I).
A profile of Egypt present and past leads viewers into the story of the search for King Tut's tomb and its excavation. Striking photos of the treasure mix with those of the original expedition to create an exciting sense of adventure and discovery.

72 TWO ROMAN MICE. Educational Enrichment. 1980. 1 fs, 52 fr. with cassette. 6:30 min. Random House. (P-I). No longer available.

This filmstrip adaptation of Marilynne Roach's illustrated retelling (Crowell, 1975) of Horace's fable, later known as "Town Mouse and Country Mouse," adds soft pastel color to the original black-and-white illustrations, lending interest and focus to the Roman setting, rich with authentic details.

73 UNCLE TIMOTHY'S TRAVIATA. Random House. 1977. 1 fs, 45 fr. with cassette. 7 min. Random House. (P). No longer available.
The lighthearted spirit of Uncle Timothy and his unusual homemade car created in Fernando Krahn's book (Delacorte, 1967) is maintained and extended in this adaptation that features black-and-white cartoonlike drawings frequently highlighted with color. Sprightly music is artfully paced with the illustrations, and the narrator reads the rhyming text with exactly the right combination of seriousness and humor.

74 THE VELVETEEN RABBIT. Miller-Brody. 1976. (394-78288). 2 fs, 77 fr./51 fr. with 2 cassettes. 14:05 min./10:10 min. $48.75. Random House. (P-I).
In this outstanding filmstrip adaptation of Margery Williams's classic fantasy (Doubleday, 1958), the rich voice of actress Eva LeGallienne and numerous new colorful drawings transcend the sentimentality inherent in the book.

75 A VISIT TO WILLIAM BLAKE'S INN: POEMS FOR INNOCENT AND EXPERIENCED TRAVELERS. Random House/Miller-Brody. 1982. (676-30169). 1 fs, 151 fr. with cassette. 17:10 min. $30. Random House. (P-I).
Through a selection of Nancy Willard's lyrical poems from the book of the same title (Harcourt, 1981), the fantastic guests in Blake's imaginary inn gleefully interact. The delightful poems are captivatingly read and sung and an original score highlights the filmstrip. The Provensens' whimsical artwork from the Newbery Medal and Caldecott Honor Book further enhances the filmstrip.

76 WE CAN'T SLEEP. Random House. 1985. (537-69020-4). 1 fs, 77 fr. with cassette. 8:05 min. $26. Random House. (Pr-P).
When Mary Ann and Louie can't sleep, Grandpa offers to tell them a bedtime story, but his tall tale seems designed to induce excitement rather than slumber. James Stevenson's (Greenwillow, 1982) cartoon-style sketches, which suit the filmstrip format perfectly, flow across the screen in a spirited adventure. The exaggerated humor of the watercolor drawings contrasts with the deliberately matter-of-fact voice of the narrator.

77 WHAT IS A FAMILY? From My Family and Me series. Encyclopaedia Britannica Educational Corporation. (24296K). 1 fs, 71 fr. with cassette. 6:56 min. $35. Encyclopaedia Britannica Educational Corporation. (P-I).
Seven children from multicultural backgrounds introduce their families, which illustrate the diversity of American family life. The factors of adoption, divorce, remarriage, multi-generational households, and a physical handicap are described through candid photography, and present a positive but realistic picture of American family life.

78 WHEN I WAS YOUNG IN THE MOUNTAINS. Random House/Miller-Brody. 1983. (676-30617-9). 1 fs, 58 fr. with cassette. 6:05 min. $27.50. Random House. (Pr-P).
A grandmother reminisces about the warmth and gentleness of her childhood in the Appalachian Mountains of West Virginia in this adaptation of Cynthia Rylant's Caldecott Honor Book (Dutton, 1982). The music, text, and Diane Goode's illustrations recreate the special quality of the relationship between the characters in a natural and unsentimental manner.

79 WOODWORKING POWER TOOLS. RMI Media Productions. 1978. (CS5-130). 7 fs, av. 75 fr. ea. with 7 cassettes. Av. 18 min. ea. $252. Charles Clark Company, Inc. (I-J).
Safe use of power tools for beginning woodworkers is the prevailing message in this carefully planned introduction to the use of the lathe, router, plane, drilling and sanding machines, and circular, band, jig, and saber saws. Sparkling clear photographs help to make this a most useful teaching supplement in industrial arts classes.

80 THE WOUNDED BUTTERFLY. Miller-Brody. 1978. (394-66235-0). 1 fs, 70 fr. with cassette. 7 min. $25. Random House. (P-I-J).
In this outstanding title from an excellent four-part series, Jean George relates the life cycle of the monarch butterfly while heightening the drama of nature with an episode involving a transplant for an injured wing. Striking pictures are provided by wildlife photographer Robert Buchanan.

Notable Recordings

1 AFRICAN SONGS AND RHYTHMS FOR CHILDREN. Recorded and annotated by Dr. W. K. Amoaku. Folkways. 1978. Phonodisc (FC7844) $9.98. Folkways. (P-I).

Rhythmic, haunting, and joyous chants encourage participation by children of all ages.

2 ALERTA SINGS. Performed by Suni Paz and friends. Folkways. 1980. Phonodisc (FC7830) $9.98. 47 min. Folkways. (P-I-J).

Children's songs from Latin America, the Caribbean, and the United States are sung in English and Spanish.

3 ANNE FRANK, DIARY OF A YOUNG GIRL. Read by Claire Bloom. Caedmon. 1976. Phonodisc (TC1522) $8.98; cassette (CDL51522 or CP1522) $8.98. Caedmon. (J).

Claire Bloom reads poignant selections from the moving diary (Scribner, 1952) of the talented young Jewish girl in hiding from the Nazis.

4 ANNIE AND THE OLD ONE. By Miska Miles. Random House. 1979. Phonodisc (394-76917-1) $10.95; cassette (394-76918-X) $10.95. 18 min. Random House. (P-I)

This gentle, thought-provoking story (Little, 1971), a Newbery Honor Book, tells of young Annie's difficulty in accepting her grandmother's certain death. Authentic music blends into the narration.

5 BABYSONG. Performed by Hap and Martha Palmer. Educational Activities. 1983. Phonodisc (AR713) $9.95; cassette (AC713) $9.95. 31 min. Educational Activities. (Pr).

Jazz music and simple rock 'n' roll, performed by Hap and

Martha Palmer, add pizzazz to everyday activities in the life of a very young child.

6 A BARGAIN FOR FRANCES AND OTHER FRANCES STORIES. By Russell Hoban. Read by Glynis Johns. Caedmon. 1977. Phonodisc (TC1547); cassette (CDL51547) $8.98. 41:16 min. Caedmon. (Pr-P).
Glynis Johns presents a charming combination of songs and stories about Frances and her relationships with parents and friends. The selections include the title story (Harper, 1970), Best Friends for Frances (Harper, 1969), and Egg Thoughts and Other Songs of Frances (Harper, 1972).

7 BE A FROG, A BIRD, OR A TREE. Performed by Rachel Carr. Educational Activities. 1976. Phonodisc (AR574) $13.95. 30 min. Educational Activities. (P).
Yoga is made interesting and fun for children; through relaxing music and Carr's calm voice, listeners are led into fourteen yoga postures. The recording is based on the book of the same name (Doubleday, 1973) by Rachel Carr.

8 THE BEE, THE HARP, THE MOUSE, AND THE BUM-CLOCK AND OTHER TALES. Read and produced by Gwenda Ledbetter. 1985. Cassette $8. 42 min. Gwenda Ledbetter. (P-I).
The warm musical voice of North Carolina storyteller Gwenda Ledbetter is well-suited to the telling of four "transformation tales" including the title story, "Tom Tit Tot," "Molly Whuppie," and "In the Beginning." Incidental music by Howard Hanger adds effective background to the dramatic tellings.

9 BILLY THE KID IN SONG AND STORY. Performed by Oscar Brand. Caedmon. 1977. Cassette (CDL51552) $8.98. 39:58 min. Caedmon. (P-I).
A story framework of the life of Billy the Kid surrounds songs of the cowboy era.

10 BORN TO ADD. Sesame Street Records. 1983. Phonodisc (CTW 22104); cassette (C5104). 31:09 min. Sesame Street Records. (Pr-P). No longer available.
Sesame Street's Cobble Stones, the Alpha Beats, the Beetles, and the Honkers perform rollicking parodies of thirteen favorite rock-and-roll hits by such headliners as Bruce Springsteen, the Beatles, and the Rolling Stones.

11 THE BORROWERS. By Mary Norton. Read by Claire Bloom. Caedmon. 1974. Phonodisc (TC1459) $8.98; cassette (CP1459 or CDL51459) $8.98. 67 min. Caedmon. (P-I).
Background music and clock chimes add nicely to the portrayal of this favorite story (Harcourt, 1953) of Pod, Homily, and Arietty Clock.

12 BRER RABBIT STORIES. Performed by Jackie Torrence. Weston Woods. Phonodisc (WW725) $9; cassette (WW725C) $9. 35 min. Weston Woods. (P-I).
"The Wonderful Tar Baby" is one of the five classic Uncle Remus tales retold by master storyteller Jackie Torrence. In a modified dialect, she provides a lively, humorous rendition of the stories.

13 BUNNICULA: A RABBIT TALE OF MYSTERY. By Deborah and James Howe. Read by Lou Jacobi. Caedmon. 1981. Phonodisc (TC1700) $8.98; cassette (CP1700) $8.98. 60 min. Caedmon. (I-J).
Harold the dog relates the story of the rabbit, Bunnicula, and his Dracula-like habits. Lou Jacobi's droll voice and amusing accent enrich this effective abridgment of the Howes' novel (Atheneum, 1979).

14 THE BUTTERFLY BALL AND THE GRASSHOPPER FEAST. Argo/London. 1976. (LSW 557/8). Argo/London. (I-J). No longer available.
A very contemporary Beatle-like score mixes well with this Victorian story.

15 BY THE SHORES OF SILVER LAKE. By Laura Ingalls Wilder. Random House. 1979. Phonodisc (394-77268-7); cassette (394-77269-5). 43:52 min. Random House. (I-J). No longer available.
New adventures await the Ingalls family as they move further west, this time to the Dakota territory. This absorbing adaptation clearly presents a segment of the author's pioneer childhood taken from her book (Harper, 1953).

16 CABBAGE SOUP. Performed by The Children's Radio Theater. A Gentle Wind. 1983. Cassette (GW1024) $6.95. 55 min. A Gentle Wind. (P-I).
"Cabbage Soup," a zany rendition of "Rapunzel" and an adaptation of "Beauty and the Beast," are performed in the style of old-time radio theater, accompanied by original music.

17 CAMELS, CATS, AND RAINBOWS. Performed by Paul Strausman. A Gentle Wind. 1982. Cassette (GW1009) $6.95. 30 min. A Gentle Wind. (Pr-P).
Original songs written and performed by Paul Strausman add a pleasant balance to the silly camp songs known and loved by kids of all ages.

18 CANDY BAND SINGS GOING HOME. Performed by The Candy Band. Folkways. Phonodisc (FC7634) $9.98. 44 min. Folkways. (P-I).
The mood ranges from wistful to exuberant as the Candy Band conjures up the simple joys and experiences of childhood in a sparkling collection of original songs with roots in the folk tradition.

19 CAROL CHANNING SINGS "THE POOH SONG BOOK." Performed by Carol Channing. Caedmon. 1982. Phonodisc (TC1686) $8.98; cassette (CP1686) $8.98. 49:02 min. Caedmon. (Pr-P).
The many voices of Carol Channing add just the right amount of whimsy to the songs, stories, and hums of Pooh, taken from the Winnie the Pooh books.

20 A CHAIR FOR MY MOTHER. By Vera B. Williams. Read by Jessica L. Aufiero. Random House. 1983. Cassette/pb.book (676-30726-4) $12.65. 8 min. Random House. (Pr-P).
Based on the Caldecott Honor Book (Greenwillow, 1982), this warm sensitive story of a young girl, her mother, and her grandmother working to save enough money to buy a special chair is appropriately read by a young narrator and accompanied by original music and sound effects.

21 CHARLIE AND THE CHOCOLATE FACTORY. By Roald Dahl. Read by the author. Caedmon. 1975. Phonodisc (TC1476) $8.98; cassette (CDL51476 or CP1476) $8.98. 68 min. Caedmon. (I-J).
The skillful abridgment of the well-known story (Knopf, 1964) of Charlie and his adventures in Mr. Willy Wonka's chocolate factory is read by the author.

22 CHILLERS. Performed by The Folktellers: Connie Reagan and Barbara Freeman. Mama-T Artists. 1983. Phonodisc (MTA2) $8.95; cassette (MTA-2C) $8.98. 37:39 min. Mama-T Artists. (I-J).
Recorded live on Halloween, this collection includes a mixture of horror and humor in a treasury of traditional and obscure tales.

23 CHITTY CHITTY BANG BANG. By Ian Fleming. Read by Lionel Jeffries. Listen for Pleasure, Ltd. 1984. 2 cassettes (LFP 7098) $13.95. 120 min. Listen for Pleasure, Ltd. (I-J).
The distinctive voice of Lionel Jeffries provides just the right touch of Britishness to this action-packed abridgment of Fleming's magical story (Random House, 1964) of a once-famous racing car which charges out of the scrap heap into the lives of Commander "Crack" Pott and his eccentric family.

24 CHORAL MUSIC OF THE SEASONS. Performed by the Budapest Children's Choir. RCA Educational Records. 1975. RCA Educational Records. (I-J). No longer available.
Traditional folk and classical songs from Hungary and other countries are sung in several languages around the theme of the four seasons.

25 A CHRISTMAS CAROL. By Charles Dickens. Read by John Dando. Random House. 1982. Cassette (676-30371-4) $9.90. 61:32 min. Random House. (I-J).
This vivid rendition of the holiday classic features several descriptive passages not usually included in abridged editions.

26 A CHRISTMAS CAROL. By Charles Dickens. Read by Tom Conti. Caedmon. 1980. Phonodisc (TC1657) $8.98; cassette (CDL51657) $8.98. 56 min. Caedmon. (I-J).
The spirit of Dickens's classic story is captured perfectly by actor Tom Conti. Each character is differentiated through Conti's dramatic talent for voice change, timing, and clarity.

27 THE CHRONICLES OF NARNIA: BOOK V. THE HORSE AND HIS BOY. By C. S. Lewis. Read by Anthony Quayle. Caedmon. 1979. Cassette (CP1655) $8.98. 58 min. Caedmon. (I-J).
The superb reading of Anthony Quayle makes this abridgment of the book by C. S. Lewis (Macmillan, 1954) enchanting. Good triumphs over evil as Bree, the talking horse, and his companion, Shasta, a young boy, flee from bondage, encountering many adventures along the way.

28 THE CHRONICLES OF NARNIA: BOOK VII. THE LAST BATTLE. By C. S. Lewis. Read by Michael York. Caedmon. 1981. Cassette (CP1674) $8.98. 61 min. Caedmon. (I-J).
Actor Michael York reads an excellent abridgment of this book (Macmillan, 1956). He ardently conveys the tension of fighting

for a cause that seems doomed as well as the courage that brings about the glorious victory.

29 THE CHRONICLES OF NARNIA: BOOK VI. THE MAGICIAN'S NEPHEW. By C. S. Lewis. Read by Claire Bloom. Caedmon. 1980. Cassette (CP1660) $8.98. 59 min. Caedmon. (I-J).

Claire Bloom's adept reading of The Magician's Nephew (Macmillan, 1955) portrays the origins and creation of Narnia and includes adventures with the beautiful but evil Jadis as well as the lion Aslan, fierce and yet gentle.

30 CIRCLE AROUND. Performed and produced by Tickle Tune Typhoon. 1983. Phonodisc (LP001) $8.98; cassette (CA001) $8.98. 37:20 min. Tickle Tune Typhoon. (Pr-P).

A blend of original, traditional, and ethnic music is performed by a troupe of musical entertainers and dramatists. All selections are dedicated to bringing people together in a peaceful world.

31 THE COMPLETE ALICE IN WONDERLAND. By Lewis Carroll. Read by Christopher Plummer. Caedmon. 1985. 4 phonodiscs (SB127) $29.95; 4 cassettes (SBC127) $29.95. 163 min. Caedmon. (P-I-J).

Lewis Carroll's well-loved story is narrated by Christopher Plummer with varied and entertaining voices in this exceptional interpretation.

32 THE COURAGE OF SARAH NOBLE. By Alice Dalgliesh. Random House. 1979. Phonodisc (394-76909-0) $10.95; cassette (394-76910-4) $10.95. 48:47 min. Random House. (P-I).

This Newbery Honor Book (Scribner, 1974) is a pioneer story which portrays the adventures of young Sarah Noble and her father, who journeyed together into the wilderness of Connecticut in 1707.

33 DANCE, SING AND LISTEN AGAIN. Performed by Esther Nelson and Bruce Haack. Dimension 5. Phonodisc (D5222) $8.98. 40 min. Dimension 5. (Pr-P-I).

This creative recording features short, lively selections which stimulate the imagination with music and sound from medieval times to modern electronics.

34 THE DANCING GRANNY AND OTHER AFRICAN TALES. By Ashley Bryan. Read by the author. Caedmon. 1985. Phonodisc (TC1765) $8.98; cassette (CP1765 or CDL51765) $8.95. 45 min. Caedmon. (P-I).
With a special poetic rhythm unique to his telling style, Ashley Bryan narrates trickster tales from African cultures taken from his book (Atheneum, 1977).

35 DEAR MR. HENSHAW. By Beverly Cleary. Read by Gregory Premmer. Random House. 1984. Cassette (676-30833-3) $10.95. 34 min. Random House. (I).
The emotions and problems of ten-year-old Leigh Botts emerge through his diary and letters to his favorite author. This recording enhances the epistolary style of Cleary's Newbery Medal Book (Morrow, 1983).

36 DINOSAUR ROCK. Performed by Michele Valeri and Michael Stein. Caedmon. 1983. Phonodisc (TC1739) $8.98; cassette (CDL51739) $3.98. 45 min. Caedmon. (P-I).
This exuberant production features an imaginary journey with Professor Jones to meet Stella Stegosaurus, Leaping Lizards, and other dinosaurs, immortalized with a rock 'n' roll beat.

37 DOCTOR DESOTO. By William Steig. Read by Ian Thompson. Weston Woods. 1984. Cassette (LTR284C) $6.50. 9 min. Weston Woods. (P-I).
To the accompaniment of a subtle blend of music and sound effects, the crisp British voice of Ian Thompson relates the humorous tale of a mouse dentist and his wife who cleverly outfox a fox. The recording is based on the Newbery Honor Book (Farrar, 1982).

38 DOMINIC. By William Steig. Read by Pat Carroll. Caedmon. 1983. Phonodisc (TC1738) $8.98; cassette (CDL51738) $8.98. 42 min. Caedmon. (I-J).
Pat Carroll leads listeners down a road with the innocent Dominic who meets and outwits the rotten Doomsday Gang. This reading covers seven chapters, completing one series of adventures from the book (Farrar, 1972). The recording also includes Doctor DeSoto (Farrar, 1982) and Caleb and Kate (Farrar, 1977).

39 DRAGONSONGS. By Anne McCaffrey. Narrated by the author. Performing Arts Press. 1985. Cassette. $8.75. 30 min. Performing Arts Press. (I-J).
A deft blend of spoken words and music effectively captures the mood of McCaffrey's fantasy world of Pern.

40 EARTH MOTHER LULLABIES: VOL. 1: FROM AROUND THE WORLD. Performed by Pamela Ballingham, d'Rachael, and Ron Doering. Cross Cultural Studies Program. 1985. Cassette (EMIA) $8.98; 20% discount to libraries. 50 min. Cross Cultural Studies Program. (Pr-P).

A soprano voice, accompanied by flute, harp, mandolin, guitar, and percussion instruments, spins a dreamy mood with ten lullabies selected from various cultures, including Ethiopian, Aboriginal, Icelandic, and Iroquoian.

41 EASY DOES IT; ACTIVITY SONGS FOR BASIC MOTOR SKILL DEVELOPMENT. Performed by Hap Palmer. Educational Activities. 1977. Phonodisc (AR581) $9.95; cassette (AC581) $9.95. 30 min. Educational Activities. (Pr-P).

Simple bouncy tunes with guitar accompaniment illustrate basic concepts and encourage motor skill development.

42 ENCYCLOPEDIA BROWN SOLVES THEM ALL. By Donald Sobol. Read by Bill Griffiths. Random House. 1979. (I-J). Part 1: THE CASE OF THE MISSING CLUES. Cassette/pb.book (394-66029-3) $10.98. 10 min. Random House. Part 2: THE CASE OF THE MUSCLE MAKER. Cassette/pb.book (394-07899-3) $10.98. 8 min. Random House. Part 3: THE CASE OF SIR BISCUIT SHOOTER. Cassette/pb.book (394-66030-7) $10.98. 7 min. Random House. Part 4: THE CASE OF THE SUPER SECRET HOLD. Cassette/pb.book (394-07897-7) $10.98. 8 min. Random House.

This series features America's favorite sleuth in four mysteries. Listeners are invited to consider the clues and propose a solution before Encyclopedia reveals the answers. From the book of the same name (Nelson, 1968).

43 THE FANTASTIC MR. FOX. By Roald Dahl. Read by the author. Caedmon. 1978. Cassette (CDL51576 or CP1576) $8.98. 54:08 min. Caedmon. (P-I).

The wry and amusing tale (Knopf, 1970) of a fox who was almost, but not quite, caught by three mean and nasty farmers is dryly but zestfully read by the author.

44 FEELIN' FREE. Performed by Hap Palmer. Educational Activities. 1976. Phonodisc (AR517) $9.95; cassette (AC517) $9.95. 30 min. Educational Activities. (Pr-P).

Music, games, and movement in delightful combination help the listener develop and use language to describe places, numbers, people, etc.

45 FEELIN' GOOD. Performed by Jill Gallina. Folkways. 1981. Phonodisc (FC7450) $9.98; cassette (FC7450) $9.98. 40 min. Folkways. (P-I).
Ten original rock-style songs by Jill Gallina encourage children to take good care of their bodies and minds and feel good about themselves.

46 FIDDLE UP A TUNE. Performed by Eric Nagler. Elephant Records. 1983. Phonodisc (LFN8206) $9.98; cassette (LFN8206C) $9.98. 56 min. Silo, Inc. (P-I).
Featuring Eric Nagler on the fiddle and countless kids on such instruments as a bleach bottle banjo, spoons, combs, and tin can bongos, this cheerful "play-along" includes adaptations of well-known songs and rhymes as well as a do-it-yourself jugband booklet.

47 FIFTY SAIL ON NEWBURGH BAY. Performed by Pete Seeger and Ed Renehan. Folkways. Phonodisc (FH5257) $9.98. Folkways. (I-J).
Sixteen songs in the folk tradition portray a history of life on the Hudson River from the days of the Native Americans who discovered it to today's environmental problems.

48 FOLKTALES FROM THE PICTURE BOOK PARADE. Weston Woods. 1981. Phonodisc (WW717) $9; cassette (WW717C) $9. 40 min. Weston Woods. (Pr-P).
A selection of five folktales from various countries includes A Story, A Story (Atheneum, 1970), Suho and the White Horse (Viking, 1969), Stone Soup (Scribner, 1947), Arrow to the Sun (Viking, 1974), and The Great Big Enormous Turnip (Watts, 1969). The tales are enriched by appropriate background music and dramatic reading by Marcia Brown, Gerald McDermott, John Akar, and Charles Cioffi.

49 FOR KIDS ONLY. Performed and produced by The Howard Hanger Jazz Fantasy. 1984. Phonodisc (HHH778) $8.98; cassette (HHH778C) $8.98. 31:33 min. Howard Hanger Jazz Fantasy. (P-I-J).
This playful introduction to jazz demonstrates the varied rhythms of blues, Latin, and swing using new tunes as well as old favorites.

50 FRANCES. By Russell Hoban. Read by Glynis Johns. Caedmon. 1977. Phonodisc (TC1546) $8.98; cassette (CDL51546 or CP1546) $8.98. 44:53 min. Caedmon. (Pr-P).
Stories about that favorite badger, Frances, include Bedtime for

Frances (Harper, 1960), A Baby Sister for Frances (Harper, 1964), Bread and Jam for Frances (Harper, 1964), and A Birthday for Frances (Harper, 1968).

51 THE GHOST BELONGED TO ME. By Richard Peck. Viking/Live Oak Media. 1976. Phonodisc (670-33768-4) $9.95; cassette (670-33769-2) $9.95. 55 min. Live Oak Media. (I-J).

Alexander, Blossom, and Uncle Miles help Inez Dumaine to her final resting place in this well-dramatized version of the popular turn-of-the-century ghost story (Viking, 1975).

52 GLOOSCAP AND HIS MAGIC AND OTHER LEGENDS OF THE WABANAKI INDIANS. By Kay Hill. Read by Rita Moreno. Caedmon. 1978. Cassette (CDL51607) $8.98. 55 min. Caedmon. (I-J).

Five tales from the Wabanaki Indians of Maine and Canada feature the Great Lord Glooscap and the Wabanaki devil, Lox. Selections from the book by Kay Hill (Dodd, 1963) are superbly read by Rita Moreno.

53 THE GOBLINS AT THE BATH HOUSE. By Ruth Manning-Sanders. THE CALAMANDER CHEST. By Joseph P. Brennan. Read by Vincent Price. Caedmon. 1978. Cassette (CDL51574) $8.98. 14:52 min. Caedmon. (P-I-J).

In these two spine-tingling stories read by Vincent Price, a young woman outwits an ugly goblin intent on marrying her and a man succumbs to the long white finger with a heavy knuckle bone and black nails which beckons from the lid of the Calamander Chest.

54 GRANDMA SLID DOWN THE MOUNTAIN. Performed by Cathy Fink and friends. Rounder Records. 1985. Phonodisc (RN8010) $8.98; cassette (C-RN8010) $8.98. 40 min. Rounder Records. (P-I-J).

An upbeat approach to folk and camp songs is offered through a variety of instruments and musical styles, including a yodeling lesson and a jazzy rendition of "The Three Bears."

55 GRAVEYARD TALES. Performed by Kathryn Windham, Jackie Torrence, Laura Simms, Gayle Ross, Mary Carter Smith, and The Folktellers. NAPPS. 1984. Phonodisc (NAPPS 4) $8.95; cassette (NAPPS 4) $8.95. 44 min. National Association for the Perpetuation and Preservation of Storytelling. (I-J).

Five chilling ghost stories and one Jack Prelutsky poem are presented by participants at the National Storytelling Festival.

56 THE GREEN MAN. By Gail E. Haley. Read by the author. Weston Woods. 1980. Cassette (LTA257C) $6.50. 14 min. Weston Woods. (P-I).
Stranded in the forest, an arrogant young man acquires the techniques of survival and in so doing emerges a better person. Gail Haley reads this timeless legend from her book (Scribner, 1980) about a figure known in Europe as the lord of the forest.

57 THE HAIRY MAN AND OTHER WILD TALES. Performed by David Holt. High Windy Productions. 1981. Phonodisc (IRC1201) $9.50; cassette (IRC1201) $9.50. 43:09 min. High Windy Productions. (P-I-J).
Here is a joyful tribute to Appalachia combining a variety of musical instruments with storytelling. Much of the material is not commonly known and is enhanced by the storyteller's use of background sounds and voice changes.

58 HANS CHRISTIAN ANDERSEN IN CENTRAL PARK. Performed by Diane Wolkstein. Weston Woods. 1981. Phonodisc (WW713) $9; cassette (WW713C) $9. 53 min. Weston Woods. (P-I-J).
Diane Wolkstein, New York's official storyteller, presents a delightful collection of Andersen's enchanting tales just as she tells them in Central Park. Included are "Hans Clodhopper," "The Goblin and the Grocer," "The Ugly Duckling," "The Emperor's New Clothes," "The Nightingale," and "Dance, Dance Dolly Mine."

59 THE HEADLESS CUPID. By Zilpha K. Snyder. Random House. 1976. Phonodisc (394-77009-9) $10.95; cassette (394-77010-2) $10.95. 31:37 min. Random House. (I-J).
Fans of the supernatural will delight in this funny and mysterious story of Amanda and her introduction of the occult to her new step-family. The recording is based on the Newbery Honor Book (Atheneum, 1971).

60 HEIDI. By Johanna Spyri. Read by Petula Clark. Listen for Pleasure, Ltd. 1982. 2 cassettes (7109) $13.95. 180 min. Listen for Pleasure, Ltd. (I-J).
An excellent adaptation of this familiar childhood tale is charmingly read by Petula Clark.

61 HIGGLETY PIGGLETY POP! By Maurice Sendak. Read by Tammy Grimes. Caedmon. 1976. Cassette (CDL51519 or CP1519) $8.98. 32:07 min. Caedmon. (P-I).
Tammy Grimes reads the story of Jenny, a sheepdog who sets

out on a search for experience, from the book of the same name (Harper, 1967).

62 THE HOBBIT. By J. R. R. Tolkien. Read by Nicol Williamson. Argo/London. 1975. 4 phonodiscs (ZPL 1196-9). Argo/London. (I-J). No longer available.
Tolkien's classic tale of Bilbo Baggins is presented in this condensation with appropriately medieval musical accompaniment.

63 HOMESICK, MY OWN STORY. By Jean Fritz. Read by the author. Weston Woods. 1983. 3 cassettes (WW485C) $33. 260 min. Weston Woods. (I-J).
Homesick, My Own Story, a Newbery Honor Book (Putnam, 1982), warmly portrays the author's childhood experiences in prerevolutionary China. Hearing Jean Fritz read her autobiographical novel creates a personal bond between author and listener.

64 HONEY I LOVE. By Eloise Greenfield. Read by the author. Caedmon. 1983. Phonodisc (TC1736) $8.98; cassette (CDL51736) $8.98. 40 min. Caedmon. (Pr-P-I).
The sensitive jazz compositions of Byron Morris add a new dimension to the delightful poetry of Eloise Greenfield in a lively interpretation of poems from Honey I Love (Crowell, 1978).

65 A HORNBOOK FOR WITCHES: STORIES AND POEMS FOR HALLOWEEN. Read by Vincent Price. Caedmon. 1976. Phonodisc (TC1497) $8.98; cassette (CDL51497 or CP1497) $8.98. 58 min. Caedmon. (I-J).
Vincent Price presents a collection of stories and poems which also includes ten minutes of Frankenstein sound effects.

66 A HOUSE FOR ME. Performed by Fred Penner. Shoreline Records. Phonodisc (SL00229) $8.98; cassette (CL0029) $8.98. 33 min. A & M Records. (Pr-P-I).
Accompanied by a variety of instruments and a school chorus, Fred Penner sings seventeen traditional songs for children in his own inimitable style.

67 HOW THE HIBERNATORS CAME TO BETHLEHEM. By Norma Farber. Read by Jane Altman. Random House. 1981. Cassette (394-07559-5) $9.90. 7:14 min. Random House. (Pr-P).
The bear, the bat, the lowly snail, and all the other winter-sleeping animals are awakened as they are touched by the power

of the Star of Bethlehem so that they too may be present at the miraculous birth. The haunting sound of flutes and a gently compelling reading help to convey the mystery and wonder of this lovely Christmas story by Norma Farber (Walker, 1980).

68 HOWJADOO! Performed by John McCutcheon. Rounder Records. 1984. Phonodisc (RN8009) $8.98; cassette (C-RN8009) $8.98. 40 min. Rounder Records. (P-I-J).
A joyful collection of traditional and original songs is performed by a kids' chorus and accompanied by instruments such as a hammered dulcimer, banjo, and fiddle.

69 HUG THE EARTH. Performed and produced by Tickle Tune Typhoon. 1985. Phonodisc (TTTLP002) $8.98; cassette (TTTCA002) $8.98. 43 min. Tickle Tune Typhoon. (Pr-P).
In an upbeat and lively celebration of life through music and dance, this collection includes a few traditional and many original selections by the Tickle Tune Typhoon performers.

70 THE HUNDRED AND ONE DALMATIANS. By Dodie Smith. Read by Joanna Lumley. Listen for Pleasure, Ltd. 1984. 2 cassettes (LFP7132) $13.95. 120 min. Listen for Pleasure, Ltd. (P-I).
Joanna Lumley's refined voice provides an amusing contrast to some of the more sinister aspects of the imaginative story (Viking, 1957) of two dogs who bravely battle the evil Cruella DeVille to save their pups from becoming fur coats.

71 THE HUNDRED PENNY BOX. By Sharon Bell Mathis. Read by Alyce Webb. Random House. 1977. Cassette (394-76912-0) $10.95. 50 min. Random House. (P-I-J).
A sensitive dramatization revealing the warmth of a young boy's relationship with his 100-year-old aunt captures the regional flavor of the Newbery Honor Book (Viking, 1975).

72 HURRAY FOR CAPTAIN JANE! AND OTHER LIBERATED STORIES FOR CHILDREN. Read by Tammy Grimes. Caedmon. 1974. Phonodisc (TC1455) $8.98; cassette (CDL51455) $8.98. 57 min. Caedmon. (Pr-P).
A selection of stories and poems, including Ira Sleeps Over (Houghton, 1972), and The Sunflower Garden (Harvey House, 1969), are read with exuberance by Tammy Grimes.

73 IN SEARCH OF THE WOW WOW WIBBLE WOGGLE WAZZIE WOODLE WOO. Performed by Tim Noah. Noazart Productions. 1983. Phonodisc (NP1001) $8.98; cassette (NP1001C) $8.98. 36:22 min. Silo, Inc. (P-I).
Songwriter and performer Tim Noah enthusiastically encourages kids to explore the realm of their own imaginations through original songs set to a rock beat.

74 IT'S THE TRUTH. Performed by Rosenshontz. RS Records. 1984. Phonodisc (RS84-03) $9; cassette (RS84-03C) $9. 37 min. RS Records. (Pr-P).
Imaginative original songs are performed by Gary Rosen and Bill Shontz. The subjects are both real and fanciful--a one-shoe bear, a wild present for mother, teasing, and friendship.

75 I'VE GOT A SONG. Performed by Sandy and Caroline Paton. Folk Legacy. 1975. Phonodisc (FSK-52) $8.98; cassette (C-52) $8.98. 45 min. Folk Legacy. (Pr-P-I).
This recording presents an appealing set of sing-along folk songs including "Did You Feed My Cow?" "Move Over," and "Aiken Drum."

76 JACK AND THE BEANSTALK. Read by George Rose. Scholastic/Folkways. 1983. Cassette (0-590-60708-1). 17:16 min. Scholastic/Folkways. (Pr-P). No longer available.
The familiar tale of "Jack and the Beanstalk" takes on new luster. The polished narration of George Rose is smoothly integrated with appropriate music performed by Arthur Rubinstein.

77 JACK TALES: MORE THAN A BEANSTALK. Read by Donald Davis. Weston Woods. 1985. Phonodisc (WW727) $9; cassette (WW727C) $9. 44 min. Weston Woods. (P-I-J).
The folksy conversational style of Donald Davis enhances the homespun humor of these Jack tales: "Jack and Old Bluebeard," "Jack Tells a Story," and "Jack and the Silver Sword."

78 JAMES AND THE GIANT PEACH. By Roald Dahl. Read by the author. Caedmon. 1977. Phonodisc (TC1543) $8.98; cassette (CDL51543 or CP1543) $8.98. 62:26 min. Caedmon. (P-I).
Author Roald Dahl does a superb job of bringing characters to life in his retelling of James's fantastic voyage (Knopf, 1961).

79 JENNY AND THE CAT CLUB AND JENNY'S FIRST PARTY. By Esther Averill. Read by Tammy Grimes. Caedmon. 1978. Cassette (CDL51577) $8.98. 31 min. Caedmon. (Pr-P).

Tammy Grimes reads two of Esther Averill's stories (Harper, 1973) about the adventures of Jenny Linsky, the timid little black cat who ventures out into the world.

80 JIBBERY JIVE. Kids Records. Dove Associates. 1985. Phonodisc (KRL1015) $8.98; cassette (KRC1015) $8.98. 36 min. Dove Associates. (P-I).

For the creator of this whimsical album, "jibbery" means tongue twisters, nonsense chants, and gibberish, and "jive" is the dancing, happy, upbeat tempo. These tunes are memorable for their playful lyrics and lively musical styling.

81 JOURNEYS: PROSE WRITTEN BY CHILDREN OF THE ENGLISH SPEAKING WORLD. Edited by Richard Lewis. Read by Maureen Stapleton and Pat Hingle. Caedmon. 1974. Cassette (CDL51440) $8.98. Caedmon. (P-I-J).

Beautiful readings are given in this collection of prose (Simon & Schuster, 1969) written by children in nine different countries.

82 JULIE OF THE WOLVES. By Jean Craighead George. Read by Irene Worth. Caedmon. 1977. Cassette (CDL51534) $8.98. 60:24 min. Caedmon. (I-J).

A moving reading of this Newbery award winner (Harper, 1972) retains the lively and courageous spirit of the novel which tells the story of Miyax, the Eskimo girl caught between two cultures who survives in the Arctic wilderness with the help of a pack of wolves.

83 THE JUNGLE BOOK. By Rudyard Kipling. Read by Windsor Davies. Listen for Pleasure, Ltd. 1983. 2 cassettes (7031) $13.95. 180 min. Listen for Pleasure, Ltd. (P-I).

Seven of Kipling's stories from The Jungle Book are included in this splendid adaptation. Windsor Davies's distinct and vivid narration animates these classic tales.

84 KENNY'S WINDOW. By Maurice Sendak. Read by Tammy Grimes. Caedmon. 1977. Cassette (CDL51548 or CP1548) $8.98. 32:03 min. Caedmon. (Pr-P).

Narration by Tammy Grimes and music by Mozart highlight this story (Harper, 1956) of a little boy's fantastic conversation with a four-legged rooster.

85 KIDDING AROUND WITH CAROL CHANNING AND THE KIDS. Performed by Carol Channing and others. Caedmon. 1976. Cassette (CDL51494) $8.98. Caedmon. (Pr-P-I).

A delightful assortment of jokes, riddles, and limericks is followed by favorite songs such as "This Old Man" and "Old MacDonald Had a Farm."

86 KING OF THE CATS. By Paul Galdone. Read by Tim Sample. Weston Woods. 1984. Cassette (LTR291C) $6.50. 6 min. Weston Woods. (Pr-P).

Eerie sound effects and the drawling voice of Tim Sample result in a winning combination of humor and mystery in this retelling of a favorite American folktale (Houghton, 1980).

87 THE KING'S FIFTH. By Scott O'Dell. Random House. 1974. Cassette (394-77046-3) $10.95. 43:10 min. Random House. (I-J).

The atmosphere of sixteenth-century North America is captured through voices, music, and sound effects in this dramatization of a story about Coronado's attempt to find the fabled golden cities of Cibola. The recording is based on the Newbery Honor Book (Houghton, 1966).

88 LAND OF THE SILVER BIRCH. J & R Records. 1985. Phonodisc (JR-583) $9.98. 38 min. Silo, Inc. (P-I).

An excellent source of Canadian culture, this spirited collection of indigenous folk songs is enhanced by the clear, appealing voices of Rick and Judy Avery. Banjo, fiddle, guitar, accordion, and percussion instruments provide appropriate background music.

89 LAURA SIMMS TELLS STORIES JUST RIGHT FOR KIDS. Performed by Laura Simms. Kids Records. Phonodisc (KR1008) $9.98; cassette (KR1008C) $9.98. 38 min. Silo, Inc. (P-I).

Storyteller Laura Simms tells rich and joyful tales from other cultures. Musical accompaniment adds to the international flavor of the stories.

90 LEGENDS FROM THE BLACK TRADITION. Performed by Jackie Torrence. Weston Woods. 1982. Phonodisc (WW719) $9; cassette (WW719C) $9. 36 min. Weston Woods. (P-I).

Jackie Torrence makes the folk characters of John Henry, Annie Christmas, Stag-O-Lee, High John the Conqueror, Marie LeVeau, and Brer Rabbit come alive in her warm and vibrant presentation of these Afro-American legends.

91 A LIGHT IN THE ATTIC. By Shel Silverstein. Read by the author. Columbia Records. 1985. Phonodisc (FC40219) $10.98; cassette (FCT40219) $10.98. 36 min. CBS Records. (P-I-J).
Reading selections from his book (Harper, 1982), Shel Silverstein makes poetry come alive for listeners of all ages. The subject matter ranges from humorous to gently thoughtful, and maybe a little irreverent.

92 LITTLE HOUSE IN THE BIG WOODS. By Laura Ingalls Wilder. Random House. 1979. Phonodisc (394-77260-1); cassette (394-77261-X). 31 min. Random House. (P-I). No longer available.
An absorbing dramatization of pioneer life in Wisconsin is taken from the first of Wilder's "Little House" books (Harper, 1953).

93 LITTLE HOUSE ON THE PRAIRIE. By Laura Ingalls Wilder. Random House. 1979. Phonodisc (394-77262-8); cassette (394-77262-6). 49:10 min. Random House. (P-I). No longer available.
Second in the "Little House" series (Harper, 1953), this episode follows the Ingalls family from the "Big Woods" of Wisconsin to their new home in Kansas.

94 LOTS MORE JUNIOR JUG BAND. Kids Records. Dove Associates. 1985. Phonodisc (KRL1018) $8.98; cassette (KRC1018) $8.98. 36 min. Dove Associates. (P-I).
The Whitely family invites the listener's jugband to play along with theirs on nineteen hand-clapping, foot-stomping numbers. It includes ideas for making homemade instruments and rhythmic combinations.

95 LULLABIES FOR LITTLE DREAMERS. Performed by Kevin Roth. CMS Records, Inc. 1985. Phonodisc (CMS696) $8.98; cassette (CMSX4696) $8.98. 43 min. CMS Records. (Pr).
A combination of traditional folk songs, more recent popular songs, and original material is presented by the soothing, clear voice of Kevin Roth. His mountain dulcimer is a perfect accompaniment for these lullabies.

96 LULLABY RIVER. Written and narrated by Linda and Mimi Danly. Danly Productions. 1985. Cassette (DPC1418) $10. 30 min. Danly Productions. (Pr-P).
A quiet time of relaxation and daydreaming is experienced in this journey down Lullaby River. Against the backdrop of the gurgling river, birds, frogs, and crickets, Tucker the Turtle takes the listener through a peaceful day in the woodlands.

97 M. C. HIGGINS THE GREAT. By Virginia Hamilton. Read by the author and others. Random House. 1975. 2 phonodiscs (394-77059-5) $21.90; 2 cassettes (394-77060-9) $21.90. 39 min. Random House. (I-J).

Voices and sound effects combine to create the world of Sarah's Mountain; the author's performance as M. C.'s mother is perfect in this adaptation of the Newbery award-winning book (Macmillan, 1974).

98 MAINLY MOTHER GOOSE. SONGS AND RHYMES FOR MERRY YOUNG SOULS. Performed by Sharon, Lois, and Bram. Elephant Records. 1984. Phonodisc (LFN8409) $9.98; cassette (LFN8409C) $9.98. 48:11 min. Silo, Inc. (Pr-P).

Children and adults join together to present 61 well-known songs and rhymes set to a lively tempo. A booklet with historical material, instructions for related activities, and fingerplays accompanies the recording.

99 MR. POPPER'S PENGUINS. By Richard and Florence Atwater. Read by Jan Miner. Random House. 1975. Phonodisc (394-77071-4) $10.95; cassette (394-77072-2) $10.95. 41:05 min. Random House. (P-I).

Humor is highlighted in this fast-moving and lively dramatization of the perennially favorite story (Little, 1938) about a man who receives a penguin that changes his family's life.

100 THE MOST WONDERFUL EGG IN THE WORLD. By Helme Heine. Read by Ian Thompson. Weston Woods. 1984. Cassette (LTR297C) $6.50. 6 min. Weston Woods. (Pr-P).

Accompanied by funny sound effects, the warm voice of Ian Thompson relates the tale of three hens who vie for the honor of becoming a princess in a "can you top this?" egg-laying contest (Atheneum, 1983).

101 THE MOUSE AND HIS CHILD. By Russell Hoban. Read by Peter Ustinov. Caedmon. 1977. Cassette (CDL51550 or CP1550) $8.98. 56:13 min. Caedmon. (I-J).

The thoughtful story of how small toys and animals band together to overthrow evil and create a warm, loving home at Christmas is presented in this fast-paced abridgment of Hoban's book (Harper, 1967).

102 MY BROTHER SAM IS DEAD. By James L. and Christopher Collier. Random House. 1976. Phonodisc (394-77081-1) $10.95; cassette (394-77082-X) $10.95. 40:42 min. Random House. (I-J).
Colonial history is effectively re-created in a fine dramatization of this unforgettable war novel, a Newbery Honor Book (Four Winds, 1974).

103 NICHOLAS NICKLEBY. By Charles Dickens. Read by Roger Rees. Caedmon. 1981. Cassette (CP1702) $8.98. 54 min. Caedmon. (J).
These excerpts, chosen by Charles Dickens for his own public readings, are read exceptionally well by the actor who played the title role in the London and New York productions of Nicholas Nickleby.

104 THE NIGHTGOWN OF THE SULLEN MOON. By Nancy Willard. Read by Zoe Caldwell. Random House. 1985. Cassette (676-3105106) $8.97. 7 min. Random House. (Pr-P).
With droll humor, Zoe Caldwell narrates the story (Harcourt, 1983) of the moon whose purchase of a nightgown throws the world into confusion. Distinctive background music evokes vivid images.

105 NIGHTMARES: POEMS TO TROUBLE YOUR SLEEP. By Jack Prelutsky. Read by the author. Caedmon. 1982. Phonodisc (TC1705) $8.98; cassette (CP1705) $8.98. 41:54 min. Caedmon. (P-I).
Frightening, yet funny, poems that will chill listeners to the bone are hauntingly read by Prelutsky. Sound effects add just the right eerie touch to 24 selections from Nightmares--Poems to Trouble Your Sleep (Greenwillow, 1976) and The Headless Horseman--More Poems to Trouble Your Sleep (Greenwillow, 1980).

106 ON THE BANKS OF PLUM CREEK. By Laura Ingalls Wilder. Random House. 1979. Phonodisc (394-76897-3); cassette (394-76898-1). 44:42 min. Random House. (I-J). No longer available.
The Ingalls move to Minnesota and live in a sod dugout on the banks of Plum Creek until Pa builds a cabin. The harrowing experiences of the grasshoppers, prairie fire, and terrible blizzard strengthen Laura's pioneer spirit. This abridgment features all the highlights of the book (Harper, 1953) in the author's own words.

107 ONE LIGHT, ONE SUN. Performed by Raffi. Shoreline Records. 1985. Phonodisc (SL-0228) $8.98; cassette (CL-0228) $8.98. 34 min. A & M Records, Inc. (Pr-P).

Using an international theme and presenting both vocal and instrumental pieces, Raffi takes listeners on a musical trip around the world to show how all people are one under the sun.

108 ONE, TWO, THREE, FOUR, LOOK WHO'S COMING THROUGH THE DOOR! Performed by Sharon, Lois, and Bram. Elephant Records. 1982. Phonodisc (LFN8207) $9.98; cassette (LFN8207C) $9.98. 46 min. Silo, Inc. (P-I).

Canadian singers present a potpourri of big-band songs, children's songs in French, old favorites, and new melodies in this live concert with audience participation.

109 THE ORDINARY PRINCESS. By M. M. Kaye. Read by Carole Shelley. Caedmon. 1985. Phonodisc (TC1774) $8.98; cassette (CDL51774 or CP1774) $8.98. 49 min. Caedmon. (P-I).

Carole Shelley's narration enhances this engaging modern fairy tale (Doubleday, 1984) about a princess who receives the "gift" of being ordinary from one of her fairy godmothers at her birthday celebration.

110 OSCAR, BINGO, AND BUDDIES. Kevin Roth Music and Production. 1982. Cassette. 23 min. Rainbow Readers. (P-I). Availability unknown.

A variety of instruments is used in this collection of camp songs, folk songs, and traditional melodies. Narrator Kevin Roth's gentle voice adds to listening pleasure.

111 OSCAR BRAND CELEBRATES THE FIRST THANKSGIVING IN STORY AND SONG. Performed by Oscar Brand. Caedmon. 1978. Phonodisc (TC1513) $8.98; cassette (CDL51513) $8.98. 35 min. Caedmon. (P-I).

Accompanied by melodies of the period, Oscar Brand portrays a young man telling the story of the Pilgrims from England to Plymouth.

112 PETE SEEGER AND BROTHER KIRK VISIT SESAME STREET. Performed by Pete Seeger and Brother Kirk. Sesame Street Records. 1979. Phonodisc (CTW 22062). Sesame Street Records. (Pr-P). No longer available.

Brother Kirk's moving "Ballad of Martin Luther King" and Pete Seeger's "Garbage" (in which he is joined by Oscar the Grouch) are included in this album along with such timeless favorites as "This Land is Your Land" and "The Old Lady Who Swallowed a Fly."

113 PETER AND THE WOLF. By Serge Prokofiev. Read by Sean Connery. Performed by A. Dorati and the Royal Philharmonic Orchestra. London Records. Phonodisc (STS15592) $3.98; cassette (STS515592) $3.98. London Records. (P-I-J).

This is an outstanding version of an old favorite, greatly enhanced by Sean Connery's Scots accent.

114 PETER AND THE WOLF. By Serge Prokofiev. THE NUTCRACKER SUITE. By Peter Tchaikovsky. Read by Dudley Moore. Performed by the Boston Pops Orchestra. Philips/Polygram. 1984. Phonodisc (412556-1) $9.98; cassette (412556-4) $9.98. 48 min. Polygram. (P-I-J).

A humorous adaptation of this well-known tale is impishly narrated by Dudley Moore, accompanied by the Boston Pops. An exceptional version of "The Nutcracker" completes the set.

115 THE PHANTOM TOLLBOOTH. By Norman Juster. Read by Pat Carroll. Caedmon. 1982. Phonodisc (TC1703) $8.98; cassette (CP1703) $8.98. 51 min. Caedmon. (I-J).

An excellent abridgment of this humorous book (Random House, 1961) describes Milo's boredom which suddenly ends when he finds a surprise package in his room.

116 PIONEER WOMEN: SELECTIONS FROM THEIR JOURNALS. Read by Sandy Dennis and Eileen Heckart. Caedmon. 1974. 2 cassettes (SWC2060) $19.95. 120 min. Caedmon. (J).

Selections from the writings of pioneer women, Elenore Plaisted, Martha Summerhayes, Elinore Pruitt, and Mary Richardson Walker, are movingly and effectively read.

117 POETRY IN SONG. Performed by Bill Crofut. Crofut Productions. 1975. Crofut Productions. (I-J). Availability unknown.

Bill Crofut has created a collection of nostalgic and haunting songs by putting verse from such poets as Jarrell, Belloc, Blake, Tennyson, and Stevenson to his own folk music.

118 RAFFI'S CHRISTMAS ALBUM. Performed by Raffi. Troubadour Records. 1983. Phonodisc (SL-0026) $9; cassette (SLC-0026) $9. 30 min. A & M Records, Inc. (Pr-P-I).
This collection of traditional and original Christmas songs is presented by Raffi, a favorite Canadian musician for children.

119 THE RAINBOW KINGDOM. Performed by Paul Tracy. A Gentle Wind. 1985. Cassette (GW1032) $6.95. 38 min. A Gentle Wind. (Pr-P-I).
A brilliantly funny collection of songs will have the listener laughing and singing and laughing some more. "Yukky" and "The Ugly Song" may become children's favorites with their clever and hilarious lyrics.

120 RAMONA QUIMBY, AGE 8. By Beverly Cleary. Random House. 1981. Cassette (394-07744-X) $10.95. 22 min. Random House. (P-I).
In a lively dramatization of the Newbery Honor Book (Morrow, 1981), Ramona deals with a new school and typical third-grade problems in her own unique style.

121 RAMONA THE BRAVE. By Beverly Cleary. Random House. 1980. Cassette (394-64517-0) $9.90. 21:20 min. Random House. (P-I).
Ramona braves spineless gorillas, first grade, and a growling dog in this engaging adaptation of Cleary's popular book (Morrow, 1975).

122 REALLY ROSIE. Performed by Carole King. CBS. 1981. Phonodisc (PE 34955) $8.98; cassette (PET 34955) $8.98. 59 min. CBS Records. (Pr-P).
The original soundtrack of the television special based on the books of Maurice Sendak presents Rosie, a would-be star, who persuades her neighborhood friends to act in her own movie.

123 THE REASON I LIKE CHOCOLATE AND OTHER CHILDREN'S POEMS. By Nikki Giovanni. Read by the author. CBS. 1976. Phonodisc (FC7775) $9.98. CBS Records. (P-I-J).
Twenty-eight poems bring to life the feelings and remembrances of childhood.

124 REBECCA OF SUNNYBROOK FARM. By Kate Douglas Wiggin. Read by Julie Harris. Caedmon. 1980. Cassette (CDL51637) $8.98. 48:39 min. Caedmon. (P-I).
In a memorable performance Julie Harris brings new life to the

times and trials of young Rebecca, who must grapple with the restrictions that respectability and the privilege of living in her aunt's home bring.

125 RHYTHM AND RHYMES. Performed by Josh Greenberg. A Gentle Wind. 1982. Cassette (GW1008) $6.95. 30 min. A Gentle Wind. (P-I).
Jazz and rhythm and blues accompany familiar songs ranging from "Brother John" to "This Old Man."

126 ROCK OF YOUNG AGES: ROCK 'N' ROLL CHILDREN CAN CALL THEIR OWN. Performed by Steve Zaldin. Zalstar Records. 1981. Phonodisc (ZRS 71051) $9.50; cassette (ZRC 71051) $9.50. 31 min. Zalstar Records. (Pr-P-I).
The lyrics of this lively offering deal with the experiences of young children and are set to an exciting rock 'n' roll beat.

127 ROSENSHONTZ TICKLES YOU. Performed by Rosenshontz. RS Records. 1980. Phonodisc (RS80-01) $9; cassette (RS80-01C) $9. 42 min. RS Records. (Pr-P-I).
Rosenshontz's enthusiastic delivery is portrayed through original as well as traditional songs which blend a variety of musical instruments and styles with humor, harmony, and versatility.

128 A SALMON FOR SIMON. By Betty Waterton. Weston Woods. Cassette (LTR256C) $6.50. 12 min. Weston Woods. (Pr-P).
In this appealing story (Atheneum, 1980), a Canadian Indian boy, after waiting all summer to catch a salmon, finds a way to rescue the beautiful fish which has been caught by an eagle.

129 THE SECRET GARDEN. By Frances Hodgson Burnett. Read by Claire Bloom. Caedmon. 1976. Phonodisc (TC1463) $8.98; cassette (CDL51463 or CP1463) $8.98. 64:29 min. Caedmon. (I-J).
In her elegant English accent, Claire Bloom reads excerpts from this children's classic (Lippincott, 1962). Varying dialects for the characters make each one come alive.

130 SHADOW. By Blaise Cendrars. Read by Marcia Brown. Weston Woods. 1983. Cassette (LTR282C) $6.50. 9 min. Weston Woods. (P-I).
Illustrator Marcia Brown dramatically reads from her Caldecott award-winning book (Scribner, 1982) as the accompanying music swells and ebbs, evoking Shadow's eerie presence.

131 SHARE IT. Performed by Rosenshontz. RS Records. 1982. Phonodisc (RS82-02) $9; cassette (RS82-02C) $9. 39 min. RS Records. (Pr-P-I).
Gary Rosen and Bill Shontz share their exuberance in a concert of original children's songs set to a variety of musical rhythms from the blues to rock 'n' roll and from a calypso beat to a mandolin waltz.

132 THE SILVER COW. By Susan Cooper. Read by Neil Innes. Weston Woods. Cassette (LTR309C) $6.50. 11 min. Weston Woods. (P-I).
In a quiet, dramatic voice Neil Innes narrates Susan Cooper's fanciful Welsh tale (Atheneum, 1983) of the wee folk's gift of a silver cow to a young farm lad. Lovely orchestral background music lends a romantic touch to this haunting tale.

133 SING CHILDREN SING: SONGS OF ISRAEL. Performed by Pa'amonim Tav La-Taf. Caedmon. 1980. Phonodisc (TC1672) $8.98; cassette (CDL51672) $8.98. 34 min. Caedmon. (P-I).
An appealing contribution to cultural understanding and musical enjoyment, traditional and original music performed by the children's chorus and orchestra celebrates the life of the child in Israel. An English translation of the songs is included.

134 SING CHILDREN SING: SONGS OF ITALY. Performed by Piccolo Coro dell'Antoniano. Caedmon. 1981. Phonodisc (TC1697) $8.98; cassette (CDL51697) $8.98. 46 min. Caedmon. (P-I).
Traditional and original Italian songs for children sung by the crystal-clear voices of a children's chorus are culturally enriching, beautiful, and fun. Bilingual lyrics are included.

135 SING CHILDREN SING: SONGS OF MEXICO. Performed by Ninos Cantores de la Ciudad de Mexico. Caedmon. 1979. Phonodisc (TC1645) $8.98; cassette (CDL51645) $8.98. 23 min. Caedmon. (P-I).
The cultural diversity of Mexico is introduced through instrumental music and songs sung by a children's chorus.

136 SING CHILDREN SING: SONGS OF THE UNITED STATES. Performed by the New York City Opera Children's Chorus. Caedmon. 1977. Phonodisc (TC1558) $8.98; cassette (CDL51558) $8.98. 39:20 min. Caedmon. (P-I).
The New York City Opera Children's Chorus sings lilting folk songs with traditional arrangements. Selections include "Erie

Canal," "Shenandoah," "Blue Tail Fly," "Simple Gifts," and others.

137 SINGING GAMES. Performed by Sally Blackburn and David White. Tom Thumb Music. 1982. Phonodisc (T321) $9.98. 26 min. Cheviot Corp. (Pr-P).
This excellent activity record for teaching and performing sixteen traditional singing games from around the world includes "Skip to My Lou," "Hokey Pokey," and "Annie Goes to the Cabbage Patch." Lyrics and game directions are included.

138 THE SNOWMAN. Words and music by Howard Blake. Read by Bernard Cribbins. CBS. Phonodisc (FM39216) $10.98; cassette (FM39216) $10.98. 50 min. CBS Records. (P-I).
Bernard Cribbins narrates the story of a boy who goes on a magical journey with his snowman. The reading is set against the musical background composed by Howard Blake for the film based on the picture book by Raymond Briggs (Random House, 1978).

139 SONGS FOR KIDS. Performed by Dick Tarrier, Jenny Cleland,/and the Swamp Cats Band. Wheatland Music Organization. 1979. Phonodisc (WLP003) $8. 38:15 min. Wheatland Music Organization. (Pr-P).
A collection of old-time songs for young children is accompanied by banjo, mandolin, guitar, fiddle, and bass.

140 SONGSPINNER: FOLKTALES AND FABLES SUNG AND TOLD. Performed by Heather Forest. Weston Woods. 1982. Phonodisc (WW721) $9; cassette (WW721C) $9. 41:39 min. Weston Woods. (P-I).
Heather Forest spins tales from Africa, Japan, and Haiti using poetry, music, and song in exquisite adaptations.

141 THE SORCERER'S APPRENTICE. By Paul Dukas. Performed by the London Philharmonic. London/Polygram. Phonodisc (STS15592) $3.98; cassette (STS5-15592) $3.98. London Records. (P-I-J).
Dukas's familiar tone poem is brought to life by the London Philharmonic. Dukas's Symphony in C Major is also included on the album.

142 SPECIAL DELIVERY. Performed by Fred Penner. Troubadour Records. 1983. Phonodisc (SL-0027) $9; cassette (SLC-0027) $9. 35 min. A & M Records, Inc. (Pr-P-I).

Canadian Fred Penner presents an exuberant collection of original and traditional songs for children, including two in French.

143 STEP IT DOWN: GAMES FOR CHILDREN. Performed by Bessie Jones. Rounder Records. Phonodisc (8004) $8.98; cassette (8004) $8.98. 38:50 min. Rounder Records. (P-I).

Bessie Jones presents a joyful collection of songs, chants, and games, rich in rhythm, from the Georgia Sea Islands and Southern states. A booklet of lyrics and background information is included in this generous example of the Afro-American oral tradition.

144 THE STORY LADY. Performed by Jackie Torrence. Weston Woods. 1982. Phonodisc (WW720) $9; cassette (WW720C) $9. 46 min. Weston Woods. (P-I).

Jackie Torrence spins tales of ghosts and varmints in these lively and compelling interpretations of "Jack and the Varmints," "Tilly," "Brer Possum's Dilemma," and "Kate the Bell Witch of Tennessee."

145 THE STORY OF BABAR. By Jean de Brunhoff. Read by Louis Jourdan. Caedmon. 1975. Phonodisc (TC1486) $8.98; cassette (CP1486) $8.98. 16:25 min. Caedmon. (Pr-P).

The beloved tale (Random House, 1933) of Babar, the elephant king, is made all the more special by Louis Jourdan's charming narration with musical accompaniment.

146 STORY OF SLEEPING BEAUTY. By Ward Botsford. Read by Claire Bloom. Caedmon. 1979. Phonodisc (TC1646) $8.98; cassette (CP1646) $8.98. 51 min. Caedmon. (P-I-J).

An exquisite retelling of this classical fairy tale is set against the background of Tchaikovsky's music. The ballet score heightens the fantasy and complements the narrator's subtle voice change for each character.

147 STORY OF STAR WARS. Twentieth Century. 1977. Phonodisc (T-550). 50:21 min. Twentieth Century. (P-I). No longer available.

A stirring narration combined with the movie soundtrack effectively stands alone without the visual effects.

148 STORY OF SWAN LAKE. By Ward Botsford. Read by Claire Bloom. Caedmon. 1981. Phonodisc (TC1673) $8.98; cassette (CDL51673) $8.98. 61 min. Caedmon. (P-I-J).

Claire Bloom reads a romantic retelling by Ward Botsford of the ballet story accompanied by Tchaikovsky's music, which heightens the intensity of the drama.

149 STORY OF THE NUTCRACKER. By E. T. A. Hoffmann. Read by Claire Bloom. Caedmon. 1977. Phonodisc (TC1524) $8.98; cassette (CDL51524 or CP1524) $8.98. 53:22 min. Caedmon. (P-I-J).

Hoffmann's original tale and Tchaikovsky's well-loved music have been beautifully meshed--the music serving as both background and action.

150 STREGA NONA. By Tomie dePaola. Read by Peter Hawkins. Weston Woods. 1977. Cassette (LRT198C) $6.50. 8:21 min. Weston Woods. (Pr-P).

The lively blend of an accordion, jaw harp, and choral singing re-creates the atmosphere of an Italian operetta in this story about Strega Nona and her bumbling assistant, Big Anthony, retold from Tomie dePaola's Caldecott Honor Book (Prentice, 1975).

151 STREGA NONA'S MAGIC LESSONS AND OTHER STORIES. By Tomie dePaola. Read by Tammy Grimes. Caedmon. 1983. Phonodisc (TC1714) $8.98; cassette (CDL51714) $8.98. 60 min. Caedmon. (Pr-P).

Ranging from the humor and magic of the Strega Nona tales to the tenderness of Nana Upstairs and Nana Downstairs (Putnam, 1973), the seven stories in this delightful collection provide a wonderful introduction to dePaola's multifaceted talents.

152 SUGARING TIME. By Kathryn Lasky. Random House. 1985. Cassette (676-31007-X) $10.95. 23 min. Random House. (P-I).

This fascinating account of the harvesting of maple syrup on a Vermont farm is enhanced by lovely background music and authentic sound effects. The recording is based on the Newbery Honor Book (Macmillan, 1983).

153 TAILS AND CHILDHOOD. Read by Michael Parent. Weston Woods. 1985. Phonodisc (WW731) $9; cassette (WW731C) $9. 42 min. Weston Woods. (P-I).

In a strong, distinctive voice, Michael Parent relates two traditional tales of "tails" and two original stories about Angela, the Mud Girl, and Martha and her kite.

154 THE TALE OF THE FLOPSY BUNNIES AND FIVE OTHER STORIES BY BEATRIX POTTER. Read by Claire Bloom. Caedmon. 1985. Phonodisc (TC1761) $8.98; cassette (CDL51761 or CP1761) $8.98. 38 min. Caedmon. (Pr-P).

In a poignant and distinctive style, actress Claire Bloom recounts six Beatrix Potter stories: The Tale of Jemima Puddle Duck (Warne, 1908), The Tale of Tom Kitten (Warne, 1907), The Tale of Miss Moppet, The Tale of Mrs. Tittlemouse (Warne, 1910), The Story of a Fierce Bad Rabbit (Warne, 1906), and the title story (Warne, 1909).

155 TALES FOR SCARY TIMES. Read by Jackie Torrence. Earwig Music. Phonodisc (LPS 4908) $9.98; cassette (4908C) $9.98. 48 min. Earwig Music. (I-J).

Four scary stories--"Elvira and Henry," "Lydia," "The Golden Arm," and "Sleeping Sickness," as well as a minute-long instruction on how to ward off unwelcome nighttime intruders--are presented by dramatic storyteller Jackie Torrence.

156 TALES OF KING ARTHUR AND HIS KNIGHTS: EXCALIBUR. By Howard Pyle. Read by Ian Richardson. Caedmon. 1975. Phonodisc (TC1462) $8.98; cassette (CDL51462) $8.98. 62:58 min. Caedmon. (I-J).

A dramatic reading from the King Arthur legends tells of Arthur's two desperate combats with the Sable Knight and King Pellinore and how he obtained the sword Excalibur.

157 TALES OF KING ARTHUR AND HIS KNIGHTS: STORY OF SIR GALAHAD. By Howard Pyle. Read by Ian Richardson. Caedmon. 1978. Cassette (CDL51625) $8.98. 60 min. Caedmon. (I-J).

From the tales of King Arthur and his knights of the Round Table, the story of Launcelot's son Sir Galahad and his search for the Holy Grail is read dramatically, conveying the excitement of his adventures.

158 TALES TO GROW ON. Performed by The Folktellers: Connie Reagan, and Barbara Freeman. Weston Woods. 1981. Phonodisc (WW711) $9; cassette (WW711C) $9. 47:40 min. Weston Woods. (P-I).

The Folktellers share their delight in storytelling in this unique blend of traditional and contemporary tales. Told solo and in tandem, these include stories, songs, and chants with an Appalachian flavor.

159 THE THIRTEEN CLOCKS. By James Thurber. Read by Peter Ustinov. Caedmon. 1979. 2 phonodiscs (TC2089) $17.96; 2 cassettes (CP2089) $17.96. 78:45 min. Caedmon. (I-J).
The whimsical fairy tale (Simon & Schuster, 1950) for older children about a cold cruel duke, the princess he imprisons, and the prince who makes a daring rescue attempt is adeptly rendered by Peter Ustinov using imaginary words that enchant and enlighten.

160 THE THREE MUSKETEERS. By Alexander Dumas. Read by Michael York. Caedmon. 1981. Cassette (CDL51692) $8.98. 60 min. Caedmon. (J).
The adventure, romance, courage, and political intrigue central to Dumas's classic tale are re-created in this effective presentation by Michael York of the first five chapters of the novel.

161 TIM ALL ALONE. By Edward Ardizzone. Weston Woods. 1980. Cassette (LTR252C) $6.50. 18 min. Weston Woods. (Pr-P).
Tim's search for his missing parents leads him along the coastal towns of England, providing adventure, suspense, and humor. The seaman's accordion and the call of the sea gulls lend a jaunty air to this rendition of Ardizzone's book (Walck, 1957).

162 TRANSPORT 7-41-R. By T. Degens. Viking/Live Oak Media. 1976. Phonodisc (670-72430-0) $9.95; cassette (670-72431-9) $9.95. 52 min. Live Oak Media. (I-J).
Effective sound effects help create a realistic atmosphere for this sensitive reading of Degens's stark post-World War II novel (Viking, 1974).

163 A TRUNK FULL OF TALES. Performed by John Dildine and Marina Cross. A Gentle Wind. 1982. Cassette (GW1016) $6.95. 45 min. A Gentle Wind. (P-I).
Amusing sound effects and a complete cast of characters accompany Dildine and Cross's rendition of Kipling's Just So Stories (Doubleday, 1946).

164 TSHINDAO AND OTHER AFRICAN FOLKTALES. By Verna Aardema. Read by Ruby Dee and Ossie Davis. Caedmon. 1975. Cassette (CDL51449) $8.98. Caedmon. (P-I).
Five folk tales from South Africa are dramatically read by actors Ruby Dee and Ossie Davis. Selections are taken from Behind the Back of the Mountain (Dial, 1973).

165 TWO HANDS HOLD THE EARTH. Performed by Sarah Pirtle. A Gentle Wind. 1984. Cassette (GW1028) $6.95. 40 min. A Gentle Wind. (Pr-P-I).
A variety of cross-cultural songs set to many rhythms, this collection includes songs and lyrics written and inspired by children.

166 TWO MELODRAMAS FOR SYNCLAVIER. Performed by Jon Appleton. Folkways. 1983. Phonodisc (FTS 37470) $10.98. 38 min. Folkways. (I-J).
Jon Appleton narrates and performs original music, composed for a digital synthesizer, that adds an element of intrigue to The Tale of William Mariner and conveys the awesomeness associated with Andersen's The Snow Queen.

167 THE VELVETEEN RABBIT. By Margery Williams. Read by Eva LeGallienne. Random House. 1975. Cassette (394-76384-X) $9.98. 24:15 min. Random House. (P-I).
The heartwarming story (Doubleday, 1958) of a velveteen rabbit that becomes real comes alive with a dramatic reading by Eva LeGallienne.

168 WHAT'S UNDER MY BED. By James Stevenson. Read by Ian Thompson. Weston Woods. 1984. Cassette (LTR299C) $6.50. 10 min. Weston Woods. (Pr-P).
Louie and Mary Ann forget their own nighttime fears as they listen to Grandpa's tale of his boyhood terrors and the prosaic causes for the many spooky occurrences. Ian Thompson humorously reads Stevenson's book (Greenwillow, 1983).

169 WHEN I WAS YOUNG IN THE MOUNTAINS. By Cynthia Rylant. Read by Ilona Dulaski. Random House. 1983. Cassette/hard-cover book (676-30728-0) $18.63. 6:05 min. Random House. (Pr-P).
Warm memories of childhood in the Appalachian Mountains are sensitively re-created by the narrator in a gentle grandmotherly voice. Original music, a blend of country and classical instruments, enhances the text (Dutton, 1982).

170 WHEN THE RAIN COMES DOWN. (Formerly: ARE YOU MY MOTHER?) Performed by Michele Valeri and Bob Devlin. C & P Potluck Records. 1977, 1984. Cassette. $9.50. C & P Potluck Records. (Pr-P).
A collection of original folk songs for young children featuring "The Bath Song" and "Dinosaurs" among others. This new edition has dropped the original title song and added a new selection.

171 WHERE THE SIDEWALK ENDS. By Shel Silverstein. Read by the author. CBS. Phonodisc (FCT39412) $10.98; cassette (FCT39412) $10.98. 38 min. CBS Records. (P-I-J).

Shel Silverstein reads his poetry with wonderfully dramatic voice and character changes, ranging from barely audible whispers to robust shouts. This recording includes 38 poems from his popular book (Harper, 1974).

172 WHERE THE WILD THINGS ARE. By Maurice Sendak. Read by Tammy Grimes. Caedmon. 1977. Phonodisc (TC1531) $8.98; cassette (CDL51531 or CP1531) $8.98. 41:51 min. Caedmon. (Pr-P).

Tammy Grimes's reading and the music of Mozart make a happy combination for the ever popular Sendak stories, including Pierre (Harper, 1962) and Chicken Soup with Rice (Harper, 1962), as well as the Caldecott award-winning title story (Harper, 1963).

173 WHY MOSQUITOES BUZZ IN PEOPLE'S EARS. By Verna Aardema. Read by James Earl Jones. Weston Woods. 1976. Cassette (LTR 199C) $6.50. 10 min. Weston Woods. (Pr-P).

This colorful cumulative African folktale, a Caldecott award winner (Dial, 1975), is read by James Earl Jones in a style reminiscent of the traditional village storyteller and enhanced by African music.

174 WHY MOSQUITOES BUZZ IN PEOPLE'S EARS. By Verna Aardema. Read by Ruby Dee and Ossie Davis. Caedmon. 1978. Phonodisc (TC1592) $8.98; cassette (CDL51592) $8.98. 38 min. Caedmon. (Pr-P).

A selection of African folk tales from Tales for the Third Ear (Dutton, 1969), including the Caldecott award-winning title story (Dial, 1975), provides an enjoyable taste of a culture rich in oral tradition.

175 WINNIE THE POOH. By A. A. Milne. Read by Norman Shelley. Argo/London. 1975. 3 phonodiscs (ZSW 537/9). Argo/London. (P-I). No longer available.

Norman Shelley presents a delightful dramatic reading of this classic story (Dutton, 1926).

176 WITCHES' BREW. Performed by Hap Palmer. Educational Activities. 1976. Phonodisc (AR576) $9.95; cassette (AC576) $9.95. 30 min. Educational Activities. (Pr-P).
A collection of songs presents a variety of concepts and language development skills and makes learning fun.

177 THE WIZ. Original cast recording. Atlantic Records. 1975. Phonodisc (SD18137) $8.98; cassette (CS18137) $8.98. Atlantic Records. (I-J).
The soul version of The Wizard of Oz is as much fun and has songs as good as the older recording with Judy Garland.

178 WOMEN OF COURAGE: IDA LEWIS. By Jeanne Hinz-Junge and Scott Hanson. Read by Theresa A. Ziegler. The Eclectic Company, Inc. 1985. Phonodisc (118W12) $4.75; cassette (118W12C) $4.75. 11 min. The Eclectic Company, Inc. (I-J).
Growing up a lighthouse child in the mid-1800s, Ida Lewis at age 14 saved four drowning men. An original shanty commemorates all eighteen of her sea rescues and the fifty years Ida tended the Lime Rock Lighthouse in Newport Harbor, Rhode Island.

179 WOMEN OF COURAGE: LIBBY RIDDLES. By Jeanne Hinz-Junge and Brian Humphrey. Read by Randy Latimer. The Eclectic Company, Inc. 1985. Phonodisc (128W14) $4.75; cassette (128W14C) $4.75. 7:21 min. The Eclectic Company, Inc. (I-J).
In 1985, the Iditarod Trail Sled Dog Race from Anchorage to Nome, Alaska, was won for the first time by a woman--Libby Riddles. Verse, narrative, and a bluesy ballad celebrate Libby, her dog team, and their 1,100-mile journey.

180 WOMEN OF COURAGE: SALLY RIDE. Performed by Paula Brandes and Theresa Ziegler. The Eclectic Company, Inc. 1984. Phonodisc (DDR106W0C3) $4.50; cassette (115CW3) $4.50. 6:53 min. The Eclectic Company, Inc. (I-J).
An exciting "You Are There" broadcast highlights Sally Ride's first space trip and includes background information about how she became an astronaut.

Directory of Distributors

A & M Records, Inc.
1416 North LaBrea Ave.
Hollywood, CA 90028

AIMS Media
6901 Woodley Avenue
Van Nuys, CA 91406-4878

Anti-Defamation League of
B'nai B'rith
823 United Nations Plaza
46 St. & 1st Avenue
New York, NY 10017

Arthur Mokin Productions,
Inc.
2900 McBride Lane
Santa Ana, CA 95401

Atlantic Records
75 Rockefeller Plaza
New York, NY 10019

Barr Films
3490 E. Foothill Blvd.
P.O. Box 5667
Pasadena, CA 91107

Beacon Films
Box 575
Norwood, MA 02062

Benchmark Films, Inc.
145 Scarborough Road
Briarcliff Manor, NY 10510

BFA Educational Media
Division of Phoenix Film &
Video
468 Park Avenue South
New York, NY 10016

Billy Budd Films
235 E. 57th Street
New York, NY 10016

C & P Potluck Records
P.O. 21075
Washington, DC 20009-0575

Caedmon
1995 Broadway
New York, NY 10023

Carousel Film and Video
241 East 34th Street
Room 304
New York, NY 10016

CBS Inc.
51 West 52nd St.
New York, NY 10019

Charles Clark Company, Inc.
168 Express Drive South
Brentwood, NY 11717

Cheviot Corporation
Whitney Building
Box 34485
Los Angeles, CA 90034

Churchill Films
662 N. Robertson Blvd.
Los Angeles, CA 90069

Clearvue, Inc.
5711 Milwaukee Avenue
Chicago, IL 60646

CMS Records
226 Washington St.
Mt. Vernon, NY 10553

Coronet Film & Video
108 Wilmot Road
Deerfield, IL 60015

CRM/McGraw-Hill Films
P.O. Box 641
Del Mar, CA 92014

Cross Cultural Studies Program
P.O. Box 43218
Tucson, AZ 85733

Danly Productions, Inc.
7609 W. Industrial Drive
Forest Park, IL 60130

Davenport Films
Box 527, Route 1
Delaplane, VA 22025

Dimension 5
P.O. Box 403
Kingsbridge Station
Bronx, NY 11520

Direct Cinema
P.O. Box 69589
Los Angeles, CA 90069

Dove Associates
P.O. Box 12196
LaJolla, CA 92037

Earwig Music Company, Inc.
1818 W. Pratt Blvd.
Chicago, IL 60626

The Eclectic Company, Inc.
261 East 5th St.
St. Paul, MN 55101

Educational Activities
Box 392
Freeport, NY 11520

Educational Dimensions Group
Box 126
Stamford, CT 06904

Encyclopaedia Britannica Educational Corporation
425 N. Michigan Avenue
Chicago, IL 60611

FilmFair Communications
10900 Ventura Blvd.
Box 1728
Studio City, CA 91604

Films, Inc.
5547 Ravenswood Ave.
Chicago, IL 60640-1199

Folk Legacy
Sharon Mountain Road
Sharon, CT 06069

Folkways Records
632 Broadway
New York, NY 10012

A Gentle Wind
Box 3103
Albany, NY 12203

Guidance Associates
Communications Park
Box 3000
Mt. Kisco, NY 10549

Gwenda Ledbetter
18 Woodcrest Road
Asheville, NC 28804

High Windy Productions
P.O. Box 553
Fairview, NC 28730

Howard Hanger Jazz Fantasy
31 Park Avenue
Asheville, NC 28801

Indiana University Audio-Visual Center
Bloomington, IN 47405

International Film Bureau
332 S. Michigan Avenue
Chicago, IL 60604

International Film Foundation
155 W. 72nd Street
New York, NY 10023

January Productions
249 Goffle Road
Box 66
Hawthorne, NJ 07507

Learning Corporation of America
c/o Simon & Schuster Communications
108 Wilmot Road
Deerfield, IL 60015

Listen for Pleasure, Ltd.
P.O. Box 588
417 Center Street
Lewiston, NY 14092

Listening Library, Inc.
P.O. Box L
Old Greenwich, CT 06870

Little Red Filmhouse
666 N. Robertson Blvd.
P.O. Box 691083
Los Angeles, CA 90069

Live Oak Media
P.O. Box 34
Over Mountain Road
Ancramdale, NY 12503

London Records
137 W. 55th St.
New York, NY 10019

Lucerne Films
37 Ground Pine Road
Morris Plains, NJ 07950

Mama-T Artists
P.O. Box 1920
Asheville, NC 28802

The Media Guild
11526 Sorrento Valley Road
Suite J
San Diego, CA 92121

MTI Teleprograms, Inc.
c/o Simon & Schuster Communications
108 Wilmot Road
Deerfield, IL 60015

National Association for the Perpetuation and Preservation of Storytelling (NAPPS)
P.O. Box 112
Jonesboro, TN 37659

National Film Board of Canada
1251 Avenue of the Americas
16th Floor
New York, NY 10020

National Geographic Society
Educational Services Dept. 84
17th & M Streets NW
Washington, DC 20036

New Day Films
22 Riverview Drive
Wayne, NJ 07470-3191

PBS Video
1320 Braddock Place
Alexandria, VA 22314-1698

Performing Arts Press
P.O. Box 3181
Taos, NM 87371

Phoenix Film & Video
468 Park Avenue South
New York, NY 10016

Pied Piper Productions
Instructional Media
P.O. Box 320
Verdugo City, CA 91046

Polygram Classics (Philips)
810 Seventh Avenue
New York, NY 10019

Pyramid Film & Video
Box 1048
Santa Monica, CA 90406

Random House School
Division
400 Hahn Road
Westminster, MD 21157

Rounder Records
1 Camp Street
Cambridge, MA 02140

RS Records
Box 651
Brattleboro, VT 05301

Silo, Inc.
P.O. Box 429
Waterbury, VT 05676

Society for Visual Education,
Inc.
Dept. BJ
1345 Diversey Parkway
Chicago, IL 60614

Spoken Arts, Inc.
P.O. Box 8791
New Rochelle, NY 10802

Sterling Educational Films
c/o Walter Reade
Organization, Inc.
711 Fifth Avenue
New York, NY 10022

Tickle Tune Typhoon
P.O. Box 15153
Seattle, WA 98115

Time-Life Video
303 E. Ohio Street
Chicago, IL 60611

Troll Associates
320 Rt. 17
Mahwah, NJ 07430

Walt Disney Educational
Media
500 S. Buena Vista Street
Burbank, CA 91521

Warner Educational
Productions
P.O. Box 8791
Fountain Valley, CA 92708

Weston Woods Studios
Weston, CT 06883

Wheatland Music Organization
P.O. Box 22
Remus, MI 49340

Wombat Productions
250 West 57th Street
Suite 916
New York, NY 10019

Zalstar
13906 Ventura Blvd.
Suite 265
Sherman Oaks, CA 91423

Index to Subjects

DEATH
Footsteps on the Ceiling, F50
Storm Boy, F131
The Street, F134
Where Is Dead? F151

DISABILITIES, PEOPLE WITH
Deaf Like Me, F38
Flowers in the Sand, F48
I'll Find a Way, F62
Itzhak Perlman--In My Case Music, F67
Sound of Sunshine, Sound of Rain, F128

EGYPT
Treasure of the Boy King Tut, FS71
ENERGY
What Energy Means, F149

ENGLAND
All at Sea, F1
Castle, F21
A Christmas Carol, R25, R26
The Highwayman, F58
Little Tim and the Brave Sea Captain, F77
Nicholas Nickleby, R103
The Secret Garden, R129
Tim All Alone, R161

ESKIMOS
Julie of the Wolves, R82
The Owl and the Lemming, FS48
Owl Who Married a Goose, F103

FABLES, FAIRY TALES AND FOLKLORE
Arrow to the Sun, F7
Bearskin, F10
The Bee, the Harp, the Mouse, and the Bumclock and Other Tales, R8
Brer Rabbit Stories, R12
Cabbage Soup, R16
Chillers, R22
The Dancing Granny and Other African Tales, R34
The Fable of He and She, F43
Fables, FS18
Flight of Icarus, F46
Folktales from the Picture Book Parade, R48
Foolish Bartek, FS20
Gilgamesh and the Monster in the Wood, FS22
Glooscap and His Magic and Other Legends of the Wabanaki Indians, R52
The Golem, FS23
Graveyard Tales, R55
The Green Man, R56
The Hairyman and Other Wild Tales, R57
Hannah and the Dog Ghost, F54
Hans Christian Andersen in Central Park, R58
Jack and the Beanstalk, R76
Jack Tales: More than a Beanstalk, R77
Journey to Moska, FS33
Katura and the Cat, F69
King of the Cats, R86
Laura Simms Tells Stories Just Right for Kids, R89
Legend of John Henry, F72
The Legend of the Bluebonnet: An Old Tale of Texas, FS34
Legends from the Black Tradition, R90
Little Red Riding Hood: A Balinese-Oregon Adaptation, F76
North American Indian Legends, F99
The Old Woman of the Mountain, FS46

Once a Mouse, FS47
The Ordinary Princess, R109
The Owl and the Lemming, FS48
Owl Who Married a Goose, F103
Shadow, FS57, R130
The Silver Cow, R132
Songspinner: Folktales and Fables Sung and Told, R140
The Stonecutter, FS63
A Story, A Story, F132
The Story Lady, R144
Story of Sleeping Beauty, R146
Strega Nona, R150
Strega Nona's Magic Lessons and Other Stories, R151
The Swineherd, F137
Tails and Childhood, R153
Taleb and His Lamb, F138
Tales of King Arthur and His Knights: Excalibur, R156
Tales of King Arthur and His Knights: Story of Sir Galahad, R157
Tales to Grow On, R158
Teeny-Tiny and the Witch Woman, F143
The Treasure, FS71
A Trunk Full of Tales, R163
Tshindao and Other African Folktales, R164
Two Melodramas for Synclavier, R166
Two Roman Mice, FS72
Why Mosquitoes Buzz in People's Ears, R173, R174
Zlateh the Goat, F158

FAMILY LIFE

Angel and Big Joe, F3
The Bamboo Brush, F9
The Bridge of Adam Rush, F15
By the Shores of Silver Lake, R15
The Cap, F19
A Chair for My Mother, FS6, R20
Children of the Fields, F26
Cornet at Night, F33
The Courage of Sarah Noble, R32
David and Dog, FS12
Dear Mr. Henshaw, FS13, R35
The Fable of He and She, F43
The Headless Cupid, R59
How Do Families Change? FS30
The Hundred Penny Box, F61, FS31, R71
It Must Be Love 'Cause I Feel So Dumb, F65
Little House in the Big Woods, R92
Little House on the Prairie, R93
M.C. Higgins the Great, R97
Me and Dad's New Wife, F83
Mighty Moose and the Quarterback Kid, F87
Mister Gimme, F90
My Brother Sam Is Dead, R102
My Mother Never Was a Kid, F94
Nikkolina, F98
On the Banks of Plum Creek, R106
The Planet of Junior Brown, FS50
Rag Tag Champs, F110
Ramona Quimby, Age 8, R120
Ramona the Brave, R121
Ramona the Pest, FS52
Rebecca of Sunnybrook Farm, R124
Sami Herders, F117
Shoeshine Girl, F120
Split Cherry Tree, F130
Storm Boy, F131
Sugaring Time, FS65, R152

We Can't Sleep, FS76
What's Under My Bed, R168
Where the Sidewalk Ends, R171

HUNGARY
Lullaby, F79

INSECTS
Butterfly, F18
Metamorphosis, F86
The Wounded Butterfly, FS80

INTERGENERATIONAL
The Bamboo Brush, F9
A Chair for My Mother, FS6, R20
A Christmas Gift, F27
Christmas Lace, F28
Footsteps on the Ceiling, F50
A Home Run for Love, F59
The Hundred Penny Box, F61, FS31, R71
It's So Nice to Have a Wolf Around the House, F66
The Lilith Summer, F74
Nikkolina, F98
Roundabout, F116
The Shopping Bag Lady, F121
A Special Trade, FS60
The Street, F134
Thank You, Ma'm, F144
When I Was Young in the Mountains, FS78, R169

ISRAEL
Sing Children Sing: Songs of Israel, R133

ITALIAN-AMERICANS
Mister Gimme, F90

ITALY
Sing Children Sing: Songs of Italy, R134
Strega Nona, R150
Strega Nona's Magic Lessons and Other Stories, R151

JAPAN
The Old Woman of the Mountain, FS46
Snow Monkeys of Japan, F124
The Stonecutter, FS63

LITERATURE
The Amazing Cosmic Awareness of Duffy Moon, F2
Anne Frank, Diary of a Young Girl, R3
The Borrowers, R11
Bunnicula: A Rabbit Tale of Mystery, R13
By the Shores of Silver Lake, R15
The Case of the Elevator Duck, F20
Charlie and the Chocolate Factory, R21
Chitty Chitty Bang Bang, R23
A Christmas Carol, R25, R26
The Chronicles of Narnia: Book V. The Horse and His Boy, R27
The Chronicles of Narnia: Book VII. The Last Battle, R28
The Chronicles of Narnia: Book VI. The Magician's Nephew, R29
The Complete Alice in Wonderland, R31
The Courage of Sarah Noble, R32
The Dancing Granny and Other African Tales, R34
Dear Mr. Henshaw, FS13, R35
Dominic, R38
Dragonsongs, R39

A Christmas Gift, F27
The Concert, F31
Cornet at Night, F33
Crac, F34
Dance, Sing and Listen Again, R33
Dinosaur Rock, R36
Feelin' Free, R44
Fiddle Up a Tune, R46
The Foolish Frog, F49
For Kids Only, R49
He Makes Me Feel like Dancin', F57
Hug the Earth, R69
Itzhak Perlman--In My Case Music, F67
Jibbery Jive, R80
Kuumba: Simon's New Sound, F71
Little Red Riding Hood: A Balinese-Oregon Adaptation, F76
Lots More Junior Jug Band, R94
The Magic Hat, F80
The Morning Spider, F92
Peter and the Wolf, R113
Peter and the Wolf and The Nutcracker Suite, R114
Really Rosie, F111, R122
The Sorcerer's Apprentice, R141
Story of Sleeping Beauty, R146
Story of Swan Lake, R148
Story of the Nutcracker, R149
Tangram, F139
The Tap Dance Kid, F140
Two Melodramas for Synclavier, R166
The Wiz, R177
Zea, F157

MYSTERY AND HORROR
The Berenstain Bears and the Spooky Old Tree, FS4
Bunnicula: A Rabbit Tale of Mystery, R13
The Case of the Elevator Duck, F20
Chillers, R22
A Dark Dark Tale, FS11
Encyclopedia Brown Solves Them All, R42
The Goblins at the Bath House, R53
Graveyard Tales, R55
Hannah and the Dog Ghost, F54
The Headless Cupid, R59
A Horn Book for Witches: Stories and Poems for Halloween, R65
The Loch Ness Monster and the Abominable Snowman; Atlantis and UFOs, FS36
Man from Nowhere, F81
Nightmares: Poems to Trouble Your Sleep, R105
Tales for Scary Times, R155
Tell-tale Heart, FS67

NATIVE AMERICANS
Annie and the Old One, R4
Arrow to the Sun, F7
Glooscap and His Magic and Other Legends of the Wabanaki Indians, R52
Journey to Moska, FS33
The Legend of the Bluebonnet: An Old Tale of Texas, FS34
North American Indian Legends, F99
A Salmon for Simon, R128

The Most Wonderful Egg in the World, R100
The Nightgown of the Sullen Moon, FS42, R104
No Roses for Harry, FS43
No School Today, FS44
Noah's Ark, FS45
Once a Mouse, FS47
Patrick, F105
Really Rosie, F111, R122
Ride the Cold Wind, FS54
Shadow, FS57, R130
Simon's Book, FS58
The Snowman, F125, R138
Steven Kellogg's Yankee Doodle, FS62
The Stonecutter, FS63
A Story, A Story, F132
The Story of Babar, R145
Strega Nona, R150
Strega Nona's Magic Lessons and Other Stories, R151
The Tale of the Flopsy Bunnies and Five Other Stories by Beatrix Potter, R154
Teeny-Tiny and the Witch Woman, F143
Ten, Nine, Eight, FS68
The Tiger Skin Rug, FS69
Tim All Alone, R161
The Treasure, FS70
Two Roman Mice, FS72
Uncle Timothy's Traviata, FS73
A Visit to William Blake's Inn: Poems for Innocent and Experienced Travelers, FS75
We Can't Sleep, FS76
What Mary Jo Shared, F150
What's Under My Bed, R168
When I Was Young in the Mountains, FS78, R169
Where the Wild Things Are, F152, R172
Why Mosquitoes Buzz in People's Ears, R173, R174

PLANTS
Legend of the Bluebonnet: An Old Tale of Texas, FS34
The Plant, F107
Sugaring Time, FS65, R152
A Swamp Ecosystem, F136
Wild Green Things in the City, F153

POETRY
The Creation, F35
The Foolish Frog, F49
Honey I Love, R64
A Hornbook for Witches: Stories and Poems for Halloween, R65
Hurray for Captain Jane! And Other Liberated Stories for Children, R72
I'm a Mammal and So Are You, F63
A Light in the Attic, R91
Lullaby, F79
Nightmares: Poems to Trouble Your Sleep, R105
Poetry Explained by Karla Kuskin, FS51
Poetry in Song, R117
The Reason I Like Chocolate and Other Children's Poems, R123
Seasons of Poetry, FS56
Shadow, FS57, R130
A Visit to William Blake's Inn: Poems for Innocent and Experienced Travelers, FS75
Where the Sidewalk Ends, R171

READING
Reading for the Fun of It: Realistic Fiction, FS53

Index to Authors

AARDEMA, VERNA
Tshindao and Other African Folktales, R164
Why Mosquitoes Buzz in People's Ears, R173, R174

ALLARD, HARRY
It's So Nice to Have a Wolf Around the House, F66

ARDIZZONE, EDWARD
Little Tim and the Brave Sea Captain, F77
Tim All Alone, R161

ASIMOV, ISAAC
The Ugly Little Boy, F146

ATWATER, RICHARD AND FLORENCE
Mr. Popper's Penguins, R99

AVERILL, ESTHER
Jenny and the Cat Club and Jenny's First Party, R79

BANG, MOLLY
The Grey Lady and the Strawberry Snatcher, FS26
Ten, Nine, Eight, FS68

BANGS, EDWARD
Steven Kellogg's Yankee Doodle, FS62

BERENDS, POLLY BERRIEN
The Case of the Elevator Duck, F20

BERENSTAIN, STAN AND JAN
The Berenstain Bears and the Spooky Old Tree, FS4

BLAKE, QUENTIN
Patrick, F105

BOND, MICHAEL
Paddington and the "Finishing Touch," F104

BRANDENBERG, FRANZ
No School Today, FS44

BRENNAN, JOSEPH P.
The Calamander Chest, R53

BRIGGS, RAYMOND
The Snowman, F125, R138

BROWN, MARCIA
Folktales from the Picture Book Parade, R48
Once a Mouse, FS47

BROWN, RUTH
A Dark Dark Tale, FS11

BRUNHOFF, JEAN DE
Babar the King, FS2
The Story of Babar, R145

BRYAN, ASHLEY
The Dancing Granny and Other African Tales, R34

BRYSON, BERNARDA
Gilgamesh and the Monster in the Wood, FS22

BULLA, CLYDE ROBERT
Shoeshine Girl, F120

BURNETT, FRANCES HODGSON
The Secret Garden, R129

CARR, RACHEL
Be a Frog, a Bird, or a Tree, R7

CARROLL, LEWIS
The Complete Alice in Wonderland, R31

CENDRARS, BLAISE
Shadow, FS57, R130

CLEARY, BEVERLY
Dear Mr. Henshaw, FS13, R35
Ramona Quimby, Age 8, R120
Ramona the Brave, R121
Ramona the Pest, FS52

CLYMER, ELEANOR
Luke Was There, F78

COHEN, BARBARA
A Home Run for Love, F59

COLLIER, JAMES L. AND CHRISTOPHER
My Brother Sam Is Dead, R102

COOPER, SUSAN
The Silver Cow, R132

DAHL, ROALD
Charlie and the Chocolate Factory, R21
The Fantastic Mr. Fox, R43
James and the Giant Peach, R78

DALGLIESH, ALICE
The Courage of Sarah Noble, R32

DEGENS, T.
Transport 7-41-R, R162

dePAOLA, TOMIE
Charlie Needs a Cloak, F24
The Clown of God, F30, FS9
The Legend of the Bluebonnet: An Old Tale of Texas, FS34
Strega Nona, R150
Strega Nona's Magic Lessons and Other Stories, R151

DICKENS, CHARLES
A Christmas Carol, R25, R26
Nicholas Nickleby, R103

DOWDEN, ANNE OPHELIA
Wild Green Things in the City, F153

DRESCHER, HENRIK
Simon's Book, FS58

DUMAS, ALEXANDER
The Three Musketeers, R160

FARBER, NORMA
How the Hibernators Came to Bethlehem, R67

FITZHUGH, LOUISE
The Tap Dance Kid, F140

FLEMING, IAN
Chitty Chitty Bang Bang, R23

FRANK, ANNE
Anne Frank: Diary of a Young Girl, R3

FREEMAN, DON
Corduroy, F32

FRITZ, JEAN
Homesick, My Own Story, R63

GALDONE, PAUL
King of the Cats, R86

GEORGE, JEAN CRAIGHEAD
Julie of the Wolves, R82

GINSBURG, MIRRA
Mushroom in the Rain, FS41

GIOVANNI, NIKKI
The Reason I Like Chocolate and Other Children's Poems, R123

GREENFIELD, ELOISE
Honey I Love, R64

HALEY, GAIL
The Green Man, R56
A Story, A Story, F132

HAMILTON, VIRGINIA
M. C. Higgins the Great, R97
The Planet of Junior Brown, FS50
Sweet Whispers, Brother Rush, FS66

HEIDE, FLORENCE PARRY
Sound of Sunshine, Sound of Rain, F128

HEINE, HELME
The Most Wonderful Egg in the World, R100

HILL, KAY
Glooscap and His Magic and Other Legends of the Wabanaki Indians, R52

HOBAN, RUSSELL
A Bargain for Frances and Other Frances Stories, R6
Frances, R50
The Mouse and His Child, R101

HOWE, DEBORAH AND JAMES
Bunnicula: A Rabbit Tale of Mystery, R13

HUGHES, LANGSTON
Thank You, Ma'm, F144

HUGHES, SHIRLEY
David and Dog, FS12

HUTCHINS, PAT
Changes, Changes, F23

IRWIN, HADLEY
The Lilith Summer, F74

ISADORA, RACHEL
Ben's Trumpet, FS3

JOHNSON, CROCKETT
Harold's Fairy Tale, F56

Index to Illustrators

ALIKI
No School Today, FS44

ARUEGO, JOSE AND
ARIANE DEWEY
Mushroom in the Rain, FS41

BOOTH, GRAHAM
Henry the Explorer, FS28

BROWN, MARCIA
Shadow, FS57

FISHER, LEONARD EVERETT
Ride the Cold Wind, FS54

FOREMAN, MICHAEL
Teeny-Tiny and the Witch
Woman, F143

GOODE, DIANE
When I Was Young in the
Mountains, FS78

GRAHAM, MARGARET BLOY
Harry by the Sea, FS27
No Roses for Harry, FS43

GUNDERSHEIMER, KAREN
A Special Trade, FS60

JAGR, MILOSLAV
The Foolish Frog, F49

KELLOGG, STEVEN
Steven Kellogg's Yankee
Doodle, FS62

MCPHAIL, DAVID
The Nightgown of the Sullen
Moon, FS42

PROVENSEN, ALICE AND
MARTIN
A Visit to William Blake's
Inn: Poems for Innocent
and Experienced Travelers,
FS75

Index to Performers

AKAR, JOHN
Folktales from the Picture Book Parade, R48

ALTMAN, JANE
How the Hibernators Came to Bethlehem, R67

APPLETON, JON
Two Melodramas for Synclavier, R166

AUFIERO, JESSICA L.
A Chair for My Mother, R20

AVERY, RICK AND JUDY
Land of the Silver Birch, R88

BALLINGHAM, PAMELA, d'RACHAEL, AND RON DOERING
Earth Mother Lullabies: Vol. 1: From Around the World, R40

BLACKBURN, SALLY AND DAVID WHITE
Singing Games, R137

BLOOM, CLAIRE
Anne Frank, Diary of a Young Girl, R3
The Borrowers, R11
The Chronicles of Narnia: Book VI. The Magician's Nephew, R29
The Secret Garden, R129
Story of Sleeping Beauty, R146
Story of Swan Lake, R148
Story of the Nutcracker, R149
The Tale of the Flopsy Bunnies and Five Other Stories by Beatrix Potter, R154

BRAND, OSCAR
Billy the Kid in Song and Story, R9
Oscar Brand Celebrates the First Thanksgiving in Story and Song, R111

BROWN, MARCIA
Folktales from the Picture Book Parade, R48
Shadow, R130

BRYAN, ASHLEY
The Dancing Granny and Other African Tales, R34

BUDAPEST CHILDREN'S CHOIR
Choral Music of the Seasons, R24

KING, CAROLE
Really Rosie, R122

LATIMER, RANDY
Women of Courage: LiBBy Riddles, R179

LEDBETTER, GWENDA
The Bee, the Harp, the Mouse, and the Bumclock and Other Tales, R8

LEGALLIENNE, EVA
The Velveteen RaBBit, R167

LUMLEY, JOANNA
The Hundred and One Dalmatians, R70

MCCAFFREY, ANNE
Dragonsongs, R39

MCCUTCHEON, JOHN
Howjadoo! R68

MCDERMOTT, GERALD
Folktales from the Picture Book Parade, R48

MINER, JAN
Mr. Popper's Penguins, R99

MOORE, DUDLEY
Peter and the Wolf and The Nutcracker Suite, R114

MORENO, RITA
Glooscap and His Magic and Other Legends of the Wabanaki Indians, R52

NAGLER, ERIC
Fiddle Up a Tune, R46

NELSON, ESTHER AND BRUCE HAACK
Dance, Sing, and Listen Again, R33

NEW YORK CITY OPERA CHILDREN'S CHORUS
Sing Children Sing: Songs of the United States, R136

NINOS CANTORES DE LA CIUDAD DE MEXICO
Sing Children Sing: Songs of Mexico, R135

NOAH, TIM
In Search of the Wow Wow Wibble Woggle Wazzie Woodle Woo, R73

PA'AMONIM TAV LA-TAF
Sing Children Sings: Songs of Israel, R133

PALMER, HAP
Babysong, R5 (with Martha Palmer)
Easy Does It, R41
Feelin' Free, R44
Witches' Brew, R176

PARENT, MICHAEL
Tails and Childhood, R153

PATON, SANDY AND CAROLINE
I've Got a Song, R75

PAZ, SUNI
Alerta Sings, R2

PENNER, FRED
A House for Me, R66
Special Delivery, R142

PICCOLO CORO DELL'ANTONIANO
Sing Children Sing: Songs of Italy, R134

PIRTLE, SARAH
Two Hands Hold the Earth, R165

PLUMMER, CHRISTOPHER
The Complete Alice in Wonderland, R31

PRELUTSKY, JACK
Nightmares: Poems to Trouble Your Sleep, R105

PREMMER, GREGORY
Dear Mr. Henshaw, R35

PRICE, VINCENT
The Calamander Chest, R53
The Goblins at the Bath House, R53
A Hornbook for Witches: Stories and Poems for Halloween, R65

QUAYLE, ANTHONY
The Chronicles of Narnia: Book V. The Horse and His Boy, R27

RAFFI
One Light, One Sun, R107
Raffi's Christmas Album, R118

REES, ROGER
Nicholas Nickleby, R103

RICHARDSON, IAN
Tales of King Arthur and His Knights: Excalibur, R156
Tales of King Arthur and His Knights: Story of Sir Galahad, R157

ROSE, GEORGE
Jack and the Beanstalk, R76

ROSENSHONTZ
It's the Truth, R74
Rosenshontz Tickles You, R127
Share It, R131

ROSS, GAYLE
Graveyard Tales, R55

ROTH, KEVIN
Lullabies for Little Dreamers, R95
Oscar, Bingo, and Buddies, R110

SAMPLE, TIM
King of the Cats, R86

SEEGER, PETE
Fifty Sail on Newburgh Bay, R47
Pete Seeger and Brother Kirk Visit Sesame Street, R112

SHARON, LOIS AND BRAM
Mainly Mother Goose: Songs and Rhymes for Merry Young Souls, R98
One, Two, Three, Four, Look Who's Coming Through the Door, R108

SHELLEY, CAROLE
The Ordinary Princess, R109

SHELLEY, NORMAN
Winnie the Pooh, R175

SILVERSTEIN, SHEL
A Light in the Attic, R91
Where the Sidewalk Ends, R171

SIMMS, LAURA
Graveyard Tales, R55
Laura Simms Tells Stories Just Right for Kids, R89

SMITH, MARY CARTER
Graveyard Tales, R55

STAPLETON, MAUREEN AND PAT HINGLE
Journeys: Prose Written by Children of the English Speaking World, R81

STRAUSMAN, PAUL
Camels, Cats, and Rainbows, R17

TARRIER, DICK, JENNY CLELAND, AND THE SWAMP CATS BAND
Songs for Kids, R139

THOMPSON, IAN
Doctor DeSoto, R37
The Most Wonderful Egg in the World, R100
What's Under My Bed, R168

TICKLE TUNE TYPHOON
Circle Around, R30
Hug the Earth, R69

TORRENCE, JACKIE
Brer Rabbit Stories, R12
Graveyard Tales, R55
Legends from the Black Tradition, R90
The Story Lady, R144
Tales for Scary Times, R155

TRACY, PAUL
The Rainbow Kingdom, R119

USTINOV, PETER
The Mouse and His Child, R101
The Thirteen Clocks, R159

VALERI, MICHELE
Dinosaur Rock, R36 (with Michael Stein)
When the Rain Comes Down, R170 (with Bob Devlin)

WEBB, ALYCE
The Hundred Penny Box, R71

WILLIAMSON, NICOL
The Hobbit, R62

WINDHAM, KATHRYN
Graveyard Tales, R55

WOLKSTEIN, DIANE
Hans Christian Andersen in Central Park, R58

WORTH, IRENE
Julie of the Wolves, R82

YORK, MICHAEL
The Chronicles of Narnia: Book VII. The Last Battle, R28
The Three Musketeers, R160

ZALDIN, STEVE
Rock of Young Ages: Rock 'n' Roll Children Can Call Their Own, R126

ZIEGLER, THERESA
Women of Courage: Ida Lewis, R178
Women of Courage: Sally Ride, R180 (with Paula Brandes)

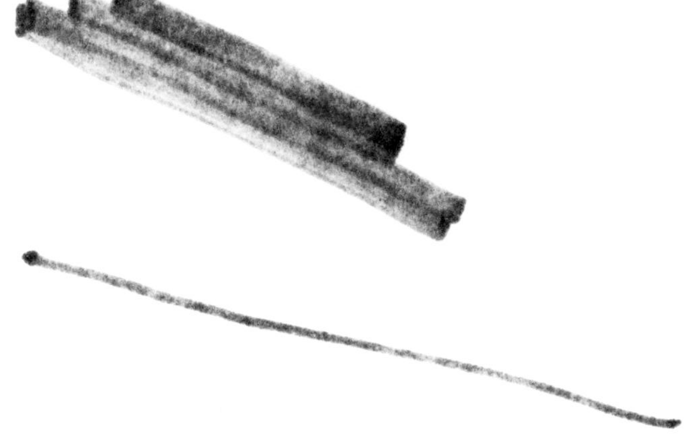

FORSYTH LIBRARY
FORT HAYS STATE UNIVERSITY
FOR USE IN LIBRARY ONLY